Thirsty

"You can lead a horse to *water*,
but you can't make him *drink*."

What is it that you *THIRST* for?

A woman at a well

By Caprice Candace
photogrphy by Jennifer Freeman

Thirsty

Trilogy Christian Publishers A Wholly Owned Subsidiary of Trinity Broadcasting Network

2442 Michelle Drive Tustin, CA 92780

Library of Congress Cataloging-in-Publication Data is available.

ISBN: 978-1-68556-093-5

E-ISBN: 978-1-68556-094-2

DEDICATION

First, in memory of my sweet friend Peggy Latham, who, in the early dawn hours before she went to work, would talk me through some of my ideas. She would help me to complete my thoughts and encourage me to put them to ink. She and I rode many trails together; she just got to the final destination before I did. Thank you, Peggy, for being such a very dear friend.

My husband, best friend, and my number one fan! Thank you for your never-ending support. I love you forever and ever. A big thank you to all our amazing adult children for their encouragement when mom felt weak in the knees!

A special thanks to Jennifer Freeman for her time and energy in putting together the great photographs for this study. She has been blessed with a special gift. I hope these images capture your heart as much as they did mine!

That all said, how can I ever thank the One who met me at the "well of forgiveness"? Who gave me the "all satisfying" living water. Who took me gently by the hand and filled my empty jar with His love. Thank You, Lord, for taking this woman at the well, teaching me to trust You through the storms of life, helping me to shake loose of the "acorns of this world," and coming into my life!

Lastly, to those of you who are on the trail: keep going, don't look back, moving always closer towards the prize... the wonderful gift of salvation!

TABLE OF CONTENTS

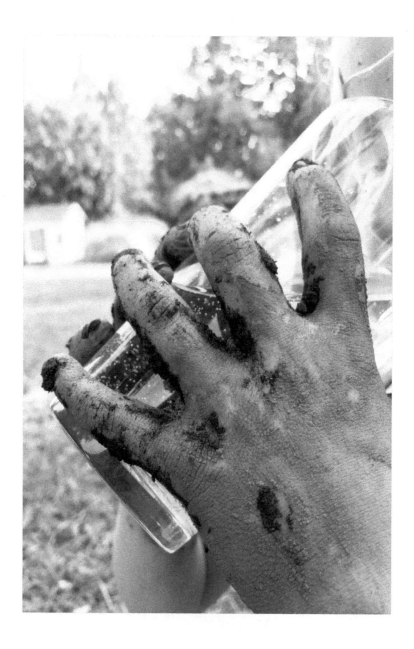

WEEK ONE

What Is It That You Thirst For?

Do you feel that you are living your life to the fullest? Or is "empty" a word that better describes your life? Come with me as we visit a woman at a well and dive into her situation and a life-changing visitor that left these words on her lips: "Come, see a man who told me everything I ever did. Could this be the Messiah?"

We are going to investigate the dynamic words of God spoken to us through the Bible. We shall explore who the woman at the well was and the impact that Jesus had on her life. In addition, we will be using the illustration of a horse and rider and what it means to connect with the Master. Here are some of the questions I hope you will discover the answers to in this six-week study: Do you have a heart for the Master? Are you empty? What do you need to fill you up? Have you been imprinted with His love? How do you know that you know God?

Too many people, as they look for the answers to a life full of "the living water" that satisfies, forget to stay connected to the source. As a small group, you will learn what the trail ahead of you holds for the believer.

Whether you have been a Christian for years or you are just starting to discover what a follower of Jesus looks like, you will have some concepts that need refining. I want you to come away from this study with a better understanding of what it means to walk the walk that Jesus intended. This study will help to develop a strong trifold relationship, you to the Lord and also to those in your life.

Every church desires to have its members acquire a situational awareness of their purpose. The correlation of this purpose is to serve others that are on the outside looking in. If the individual does not fully grasp what their role is in this mission of follower, things can get rather disjointed. Every so often, it is important to do a head-to-toe assessment of who you are in relation to the Lord. Once we discover what it is that needs adjusting and fine-tuning, we will be able to ride the trail marked out for us with wisdom and insight, encouraging others to take a closer look at who is offering the living water that satisfies Jesus, our Lord and Savior.

WEEK ONE

Heart for the Master

Day One

What are some of your favorite animals? Have you ever owned any unusual pets? How about farm or ranch animals? When we were first starting out as parents, we made the decision to home educate our five children. Looking for a better place to raise them, my husband and I made the decision to move from a valley in Southern California with a population in 1990 of over three million people to a rural ranch community in Northern California. We settled in a coastal valley with a whopping population of twenty-five. *Did she say twenty-five?* Yes, and I was indicating the number of people, not chickens. There are more animals than there are people in our little town! We dove in quickly to the ranch lifestyle, which included having up to twenty-eight horses at one time on our ranch of over 280 acres. From city dweller to country girl, I had some incredible lessons to learn.

Horses are amazing animals created by our Lord for our service. They are swift, capable of not only carrying a rider for long distances but also considered a beast of burden. In the wild, horses congregate in herds and are natural grazers. In the wild, horses roam the grasslands eating and drinking as needed. When we domesticated them, it became necessary for the animal to develop dependency upon its caregiver. This dependency is what builds the relationship between horse and rider. The key to this relationship is that the horse must develop trust in its master in order for its needs to be met. The horse will receive everything it requires from his master; a relationship of trust and commitment develops so strong that a horse can acquire a desire for his master that surpasses the herding instinct. In the horse community, we call this a "horse with heart."

We, too, have hearts that crave to belong to something great. We were designed for relationship. We call our master Lord; He is our God and the One who cares for us. And when we develop a relationship with our Master, we too receive the provision we so desperately need. When we finally drink from the "living waters" offered by our Master, we come to the understanding of what true relationship was meant to be, and our "hearts" become His.

Come with me for this six-week journey as we discover what it is that you thirst for. You have all heard the saying, "You can lead a horse to water, but you can't make it drink." You may be asking yourself, "So what is the problem with a horse that won't drink? I am sure they are smart enough to drink when they become thirsty enough." I wish that were true, but like us, they can become very ill and even die if not properly hydrated. An idle horse needs a minimum of ten gallons of water a day, and an active horse in hot weather can suck up to twenty-four gallons. So why would a horse be so stubborn to not drink water as needed? Well, just like we don't always do what is best for us, horses don't either. On our ranch, we need to make sure that the horses are drinking enough water to keep them healthy, so we create a thirst for what they need. In other words, we lure the horse to water.

As we look to the Word of God for what satisfies our thirsty souls. We are going to tether ourselves to the book of John chapter four as we unfold the dynamics of the woman at the well. We will look at what it means to be empty, dehydrated, or satisfied. We will talk about the need to trust our Lord in our circumstances, just like the horse must rely on its master. So let's saddle up for a unique journey with the woman at the well.

Read John chapter 4:1-29 (NIV):

> Now Jesus learned that the Pharisees had heard that he was gaining and baptizing more disciples than John— although in fact it was not Jesus who baptized, but his disciples. So he left Judea and went back once more to Galilee.
>
> Now he had to go through Samaria. So he came to a town in Samaria called Sychar, near the plot of ground Jacob had given to his son Joseph. Jacob's well was there, and Jesus, tired as he was from the journey, sat down by the well. It was about noon. When a Samaritan woman came to draw water, Jesus said to her, "Will you give me a drink?" (His disciples had gone into the town to buy food.)
>
> The Samaritan woman said to him, "You are a Jew and I am a Samaritan woman. How can you ask me for a drink?" (For Jews do not associate with Samaritans.)
>
> Jesus answered her, "If you knew the gift of God and who it is that asks you for a drink, you would have asked him and he would have given you living water." "Sir," the woman said, "you have nothing to draw with and the well is deep. Where can you get this living water? Are you greater than our father Jacob, who gave us the well and drank from it himself, as did also his sons and his livestock?"
>
> Jesus answered, "Everyone who drinks this water will be thirsty again, but whoever drinks the water I give them will never thirst. Indeed, the water I give them will become in them a spring of water welling up to eternal life."
>
> The woman said to him, "Sir, give me this water so that

I won't get thirsty and have to keep coming here to draw water."

He told her, "Go, call your husband and come back."

"I have no husband," she replied.

Jesus said to her, "You are right when you say you have no husband. The fact is, you have had five husbands, and the man you now have is not your husband. What you have just said is quite true."

"Sir," the woman said, "I can see that you are a prophet. Our ancestors worshiped on this mountain, but you Jews claim that the place where we must worship is in Jerusalem."

"Woman," Jesus replied, "believe me, a time is coming when you will worship the Father neither on this mountain nor in Jerusalem. You Samaritans worship what you do not know; we worship what we do know, for salvation is from the Jews. Yet a time is coming and has now come when the true worshipers will worship the Father in the Spirit and in truth, for they are the kind of worshipers the Father seeks. God is spirit, and his worshipers must worship in the Spirit and in truth."

The woman said, "I know that Messiah" (called Christ) "is coming. When he comes, he will explain everything to us."

Then Jesus declared, "I, the one speaking to you — I am he."

Just then his disciples returned and were surprised to find him talking with a woman. But no one asked, "What do you want?" or "Why are you talking with her?"

Then, leaving her water jar, the woman went back to the town and said to the people, "Come, see a man who told me everything I ever did. Could this be the Messiah?"

Today, ask God to open your heart to hear His voice as He calls you to drink from His living water.

1. List the things that you thirst for in this world.

2. What are the things of life that fill you up?

3. When was the first time you realized that you needed to listen to your Lord's call?

4. What or who is the master of your life?

5. Do you know what the gift of God is?

6. Do you consider yourself "just one of the herd," or do you have a "heart for the master"? Please explain.

Prayer:

Dear Lord, help us to draw closer to You in this journey we are about to take. Open our ears to hear Your call. And help us to develop a thirst for Your living water. In Jesus' name, amen.

WEEK ONE

Are You Connected?

Day Two

Every horseman yearns to develop a relationship with their horse, a relationship of trust and commitment. A horse with a heart for its master is a horse that wants to belong. We all have a desire to belong and feel part of something. But have you ever felt left out or like the outcast? People seem to be avoiding you for one reason or another? The woman at the well knew what this felt like. She knew isolation as a result of choices. Yet, she, too, desired to belong to something of value. Let's look to the Bible for understanding into a heart for the master.

I want to first take us on a journey with our Master as He engages the woman at the well. So let's take a closer look at John chapter four.

> Now Jesus learned that the Pharisees had heard that he was gaining and baptizing more disciples than John—although in fact it was not Jesus who baptized, but his disciples. So he left Judea and went back once more to Galilee.
> Now he had to go through Samaria. So he came to a town in Samaria called Sychar, near the plot of ground Jacob had given to his son Joseph. Jacob's well was there, and Jesus, tired as he was from the journey, sat down by the well. It was about noon.
> When a Samaritan woman came to draw water, Jesus said to her, "Will you give me a drink?" (His disciples

had gone into the town to buy food.) The Samaritan woman said to him, "You are a Jew and I am a Samaritan woman. How can you ask me for a drink?" (For Jews do not associate with Samaritans.)

John 4:1-9 (NIV)

The text opens with those record-keeping Pharisees, eyeing Jesus' every move. In verses 1-2, did you notice that they are keeping score, that they are counting the baptisms even though it was the disciples that were doing the baptizing? Take note also that they are working off of hearsay. I love how the Message says it: "They had posted the score that Jesus was ahead, turning him and John into rivals in the eyes of the people."

So our Lord Jesus decides that it is time to return to Judea, but not by the usual route traveled by the Jews. The Jews, fearing an undesirable encounter with the Samaritans, would journey the long way around and go out of their way when traveling from Galilee. They would cross over the Jordan River and travel south along the land opposite Samaria, then cross back over the river to reach Judea.

Did you notice that verse 4 states, "Now he had to go through Samaria"? This suggests that Jesus had a very special reason for choosing the route He did. Could it be that Jesus had an extraordinary mission? When He finally arrives, He is exhausted from the travel, so He sits down by the well in the heat of the noonday sun. He is alone, and the dust of His travels clings to His cloak.

Now the scene shifts focus to a Samaritan woman, not a group of women, but a woman who is alone in her quest for her daily supply of water. Could she be the object of His mission?

Could it be that He has an appointment with this woman? Jesus asks this woman for a drink. In verse 9, she replies, "You are a Jew and I am a Samaritan woman. How can you ask me for a drink?" Time to put some application to the beginning of our story.

As the Samaritan woman walks down the dusty path that leads to the well, she is probably very aware of her solitude. Having this daily routine of loneliness, it would give her the time to reflect on how she got to this station of solitude. There are no other women to share stories with while she works. She is by herself. The only sounds she hears are muffled voices behind closed doors as she exits the village.

The woman asks Jesus, "You are a Jew and I am a Samaritan woman. How can you ask me for a drink?" She is aware that the traveling stranger is from Judea, a Jew. The Jews had rituals that had to be performed before they could touch an item that became unclean. The Jews, because of religious differences, thought of the Samaritans as people who were unclean. So if this woman were to draw the water from the well and pour it into a vessel for Jesus to drink, she would have to touch the vessel and hand it to Him. This would then result in the drinking vessel becoming "unclean" in the eyes of a Jewish person. Jesus understood this, yet it did not hold Him back; He wanted to connect with this woman. Just like He wants to connect with you and me.

1. What are the things that you consider clean or unclean in your life?

2. Let's be honest with ourselves for a moment. What are the things that keep us from connecting with others?

3. Do you ever feel alone in your daily tasks?

4. What are the barriers you put in place to separate you from others that you consider different?

5. List the "no-touch zones" that you were taught growing up in your community.

Jesus had an extraordinary mission, an appointment that He didn't want to miss. Take a moment in the stillness of this study and listen. Listen carefully to your Master's call. He is waiting just like He was waiting for the Samaritan woman to come down the path on that hot afternoon. He wants to meet you and spend time with you!

"Ask, and you will receive. Search, and you will find. Knock, and the door will be opened for you. Everyone who asks will receive. Everyone who searches will find. And the door will be opened for everyone who knocks."

Matthew 7:7-8 (CEV)

Listen and be still. Write anything that comes to your mind.

1. What questions do I need to be asking?

2. I want to receive from you...

3. Lord, help me to search and find...

4. I need to walk through the door of...

5. Help me to keep knocking until I receive...

Prayer:

Dear Lord,

Help me to recognize the obstacles in my life that keep me from fully connecting with You. What is it that You want me to do in order to fully engage with You and others in my life? Give me eyes to see the hurdles in my life that I need to remove so I am no longer isolated from those that You would have me encounter. Help me to knock loudly and with determination until the door is opened, to seek You first in my life, and to allow You to fill me up! Amen.

Bucket by Bucket:
Day Three

A ranch or a farm has the need of a couple of things to
make them worthy of the work: good land and plenty of clean,
accessible water. Without water, no matter how much land you
have, you will not be able to grow anything or graze your animals.
Water that is not clean is usually not potable. Foul water has not
only a bad smell but will usually not taste good. Several years ago,
we heard of a rancher in the area that, due to a local earthquake,
had a shift in the underground water table that gravely affected
his fresh water. His water source went from sweet-smelling to the
odor of rotten eggs. Most of us would agree that would make for
some nasty refreshments.

Horses can be temperamental in their eating and drinking
habits. When you travel with them, a change in odor can make
the animal turn up his nose no matter how many times you bring
him to the water bucket. So this is where we need to "lure" them
to drink. A little apple juice or molasses can go a long way to get
a horse to drink. Salt blocks can also be of use by increasing the
actual thirst of the animal. Here we find Jesus is engaging the
woman at the well in order to increase her thirst for the
living water.

> Jesus answered her, "If you knew the gift of God and
> who it is that asks you for a drink, you would have asked
> him and he would have given you living water." "Sir," the
> woman said, "you have nothing to draw with and the

well is deep. Where can you get this living water? Are
you greater than our father Jacob, who gave us the well
and drank from it himself, as did also his sons and his
livestock?"
Jesus answered, "Everyone who drinks this water will be
thirsty again, but whoever drinks the water I give them
will never thirst. Indeed, the water I give them will
become in them a spring of water welling up to eternal
life." The woman said to him, "Sir, give me this water so
that I won't get thirsty and have to keep coming here to
draw water."

John 4:10-15 (NIV)

Ah! The gift of unmerited favor that does not require
anything from us. Why is that always such a difficult concept for
us to wrap our human brains around? And for the record, what
is this gift of living water? The water "living" in Old Testament
times pointed to Jehovah, who was referred to as "the fountain of
living waters" in Jeremiah 2:13 and sometimes referred to the Holy
Spirit. But here, the term is used to explain "eternal life."

It is intriguing to me that she either ignores or doesn't grasp
everything that He says. She responds, "Sir, you have nothing to
draw with, and the well is deep. Where can you get this living
water? Are you greater than our father Jacob, who gave us the well
and drank from it himself, as did also his sons and his livestock?"
The wells of her time and location would have been hand dug.
They were typically around a hundred feet deep. Bucket by
bucket, dirt would be removed. Deeper and deeper, the person
who was digging would be lowered. The process was laborious and
dangerous but necessary to provide fresh water in the arid land.
Once dug, the hauling up of the water took time and muscle.

Here she is, questioning Jesus against her knowledge of Jacob's well. Like the Pharisees' scorekeeping tenancies, she analyzes whose well is better. She is holding onto what she has known rather than leaning into what is before her. Remember Jesus said to her, "If you knew the gift of God and who it is that asks you for a drink, you would have asked him and he would have given you living water." Did you catch that? He, Jesus, knows the answer to what the gift is and who does the giving. He then explains to her in a way that she might be able to grasp that this water, not what is in the well before her, will forever satisfy, fulfill her needs and make her complete forever and ever. No more loneliness.

1. What holds you connected to your past?

2. What robs you from drinking the living water?

In verse 15, the woman asks, "Sir, give me this water so that I won't get thirsty and have to keep coming here to draw water." It appears that she is more concerned with the work required in the effort of daily living than the ability of the living water to sustain life. Here we have Jesus the Son of God offering rather than requiring a request for "living water." "Living" is defined as "alive, not dead, realistic, or true to life, interesting in a way that is relevant and useful, designed for living in, especially for social and recreational activities." Wow, I love this! Jesus is relevant to our generation and the woman at the well. He holds the answers, but she is still caught in her limited view; for her, it is about her work and station in life. She was designed for "living in the love of the Lord" and actively drinking from His living waters.

1. List the things in your life that seem to limit you from moving on.

2. Do you keep coming back to the well, declining to drink the water that satisfies? Are you afraid of the work it takes to draw?

3. What does unmerited favor mean to you?

4. Explain the life you are living; is it a relevant and useful life?

5. Think of someone you know that is holding onto the things that they know rather than trusting the Master. Lift them up to the Lord in prayer. Ask God to give you the opportunity to bring them to the well of "living water."

Prayer:

Dear Lord,

Will You show me more about the living water? I want to look deep into Your clear, life-giving well. Reveal to me the things that hold me tethered to the past. I no longer want to remain parched in the arid land of unbelief. Full commitment is the desire of my heart. Thank You for Your loving offer not only to the woman at the well but to me too. For reaching across the ages with the offer to drink and live! In the eternal life-giving name of Jesus, amen!

If the Truth Be Known

Day Four

In the horse world, when you go in search of a new animal, you try to discover every possible bad habit, conformation attribute, or fault, and health status of the horse. You want to expose any positive or negative aspects of the animal. That way, you can move forward with a purchase or look for a better fit for your needs.

We once bought this beautiful paint pony for our girls when they were first learning to ride. We affectionately named him Chunky due to his protruding belly. We thought we had exactly what we were looking for in an all-around pony for the girls until, one day, we went out riding in the hills. I was leading with my horse when all of a sudden, I heard my daughter let out a yelp. As I looked over my shoulder, I saw her and the pony going down. This vixen of a pony had decided that he was getting a little itchy under his saddle and that a good roll in the dusty dirt might help. The good Lord was watching over the precious cargo of my daughter that day. The only thing that happened was wisdom in how to recognize the pony's desire to roll and how to keep him moving forward on his journey down the trail. We wish we had learned this truth about this animal before we purchased him. We wanted to be able to look deep inside of every horse that came onto our ranch after this experience; into their hearts and minds regarding their bad or good habits and behaviors.

1. Are there any truths that you wished you had learned earlier in life?

2. What are those truths?

What if everyone who met you could know the truth about you? It would be daunting, intimidating, and terrifying to hear someone who you just met sitting by a well start to unfold your choices, bad habits, and behaviors in life right before you. But then again, what if it helped you to stay on your journey down the trail of life without further harm? Jesus is just about to engage this woman with some searing truths.

> He told her, "Go, call your husband and come back." "I have no husband," she replied. Jesus said to her, "You are right when you say you have no husband. The fact is, you have had five husbands, and the man you now have is not your husband. What you have just said is quite true." "Sir," the woman said, "I can see that you are a prophet. Our ancestors worshiped on this mountain, but you Jews claim that the place where we must worship is in Jerusalem."
>
> John 4:16-20 (NIV)

1. Do you wish you could be more transparent?

2. Why or why not?

Is this a test for the truth or a way to help her discover her sin? Jewish law provided a woman the ability to be divorced two to three times at the most. She had exceeded this, plus she was living with her present lover. She had an appointment with the Son of God in regards to a heart check. She even recognizes Him as gifted to be a "prophet" but challenges Him in His knowledge of religious practices.

Did you notice that she is bringing up the details of how, not the truth of "who is" to be worshiped? She is on a path of "I know what is better for you and me." So down she goes to roll in the dust of debate.

1. Do you tend to debate or listen?

2. When is it best to *listen to* verses *debate* the issues of life?

3. When was the last time you had a heart check? What were the results?

4. Does your heart need some CPR? Make a list of its needs.

    a. Care

    b. Prayer

    c. Repair

We have been given the gift of the Holy Spirit to show us when we stray off the right trail. It takes good ears to hear what the Spirit is telling us. Learning the truth about ourselves is a lot like getting older. You see, your eyes start to go, and things get fuzzy as you age. Before I put my glasses on in the morning, the image in the mirror appears rather good for "her age." But when the glasses go on, the truth be known, I am getting older. All the aging details of the human condition come glaring back at me in the reflection of time. Jesus wants to put our image through the test of His reflection.

Take a few minutes in the mirror of truth and make a list of five habits that need to be examined a little more carefully.

1.

2.

3.

4.

5.

Now, if you know the changes that need to be made in order to "get back on the right trail," do it. Otherwise, start praying for the Lord to give you insight on how to move back onto the right trail of your faith.

Prayer:

Dear Jesus,

Open my eyes to see clearly who I am. I want to reflect a life that is lived with You. I want to be able to have others see You in me by taking my list of habits and starting the process of change. Please, set me back on the right trail. Thank You for hearing the requests and questions that I speak to You in prayer. I need Your care as I am in prayer for my needed repair. Amen.

Do You See the Whole Picture?

Day Five

If I was to go to a breeding farm in the search of a good mare to purchase, I might be invited to view horses stabled in their barn. Walking down the row of stalls, I might notice a horse or two with their heads peeking out at me in curiosity.

Looking at these horses, I would take notice of the condition of their coat, their color, and facial markings, if any. If the lighting is good, I might even be able to denote clarity or even possible cloudiness of the eyes. But unless I have the owner take that horse out of the stall, I would only see part of the horse. I will tell you with all certainty that I would never invest in an animal having only seen its head.

It is also true with our faith. We need to see the whole picture. We need to peer deeply into all the aspects of our belief. The Samaritans had only accepted part of the Word of God as truth. They worshiped the One and only true God, but not in His entirety. The woman at the well continued to avoid the real issue, to see God in His totality, not just the part that was convenient.

> "Woman," Jesus replied, "believe me, a time is coming
> when you will worship the Father neither on this
> mountain nor in Jerusalem. You Samaritans worship
> what you do not know; we worship what we do know,
> for salvation is from the Jews. Yet a time is coming and
> has now come when the true worshipers will worship

the Father in the Spirit and in truth, for they are the kind of worshipers the Father seeks. God is spirit, and his worshipers must worship in the Spirit and in truth." The woman said, "I know that Messiah" (called Christ) "is coming. When he comes, he will explain everything to us." Then Jesus declared, "I, the one speaking to you—I am he." Just then his disciples returned and were surprised to find him talking with a woman. But no one asked, "What do you want?" or "Why are you talking with her?" Then, leaving her water jar, the woman went back to the town and said to the people, "Come, see a man who told me everything I ever did. Could this be the Messiah?"

John 4:21-29 (NIV)

God clearly points out in the Old Testament that He is God and we are not. He is the Creator and designer. He molds us into His design. Be careful not to try to fit God into your plan for your use. I can guarantee it doesn't go over well!

"Go to the pottery shop, and when you get there, I will tell you what to say to the people." I went there and saw the potter making clay pots on his pottery wheel. And whenever the clay would not take the shape he wanted, he would change his mind and form it into some other shape.

Jeremiah 18:2-8 (CEV)

Now we see things imperfectly as in a cloudy mirror, but then we will see everything with perfect clarity. All that I know now is partial and incomplete, but then I will know everything completely, just as God now knows me completely.

First Corinthians 13:12 (NLT)

Oh me! Oh my! She, like so many of us, is still trying to mold the concept of the Lord Almighty into her very own neat and tidy package. I will give her a little slack as we consider the historical culture of the time. So what we do know and understand about the Samaritans is that they did believe in God, our God of the Bible. Although when they considered Him as God, they gazed upon Him as a "fractured piece" that was incomplete. Let me put it this way. If you only know part of who you worship, aren't you in danger of creating something that fits your own needs for the other missing pieces? They had accepted the Pentateuch, the Torah, or the first five books of the Bible but rejected the rest. This led to multiple disagreements over the years between them and their Jewish neighbors. To the point that the Pharisees had labeled contact with the Samaritans as "unclean."

1. "Pieces"... What does your view of God look like?

2. Do you only see "fractured pieces"?

3. How do you mold the clay of life to fit your own needs, to conform to your agenda, not God's purpose?

4. What does your image of God look like?

5. What is it that you believe?

I believe...

You have some work to do as you consider the questions above. Like the woman at the well, we will spend some time getting to know Jesus:

God wants to have alone time with you.

He wants us to grab a hold of who He really is.

1. What is the condition of your heart for Jesus?

2. Are you empty, dehydrated, or satisfied?

3. Who is your God?

Thank you for joining me for this first week. We will look deeper and deeper into the well of living water as we continue to discover what it is that satisfies our thirst. I hope you stay on this trail. It is going to lead you further in your walk with God, the Lord and Redeemer, whose love sustains us with His living water.

"Come, see a man who told me everything I ever did. Could this be the Messiah?"

Prayer:

Dear Lord,

I no longer want to see You in pieces. Please help me to see the entire plan that You have for my life and me. I desire for You to be the potter and for me to be the clay. Mold and shape me into the child of God You would have me to be. In Jesus' name, amen.

WEEK TWO

The Empty Trough

Do you feel empty? Like there may be something missing in your life? Are you just maybe a little dried up? Whether you are looking into the well or leaning on your own understanding, we should take a closer look to discover who God is and what His plan is for us. Have you already connected with Jesus? Then, it is time for a review. Are you searching and debating God's plan? Then, let's look deeply into the well with intent interest to what this living water is all about.

WEEK TWO

Created

Day One

One of the most impressive things about having moved from an enormous city to the middle of nowhere is the beauty of this world. In the city, you drive on paved roads in filthy air. There is noise and congestion in every inch of space. A haunting humming of the city can be heard twenty-hour hours a day. At night the sky takes on a sort of orange glow from all of the lights, and in the day, it is just plain yucky. There is the constant scent of exhaust in your nostrils, and sometimes the air is so thick that it is difficult to breathe. The only "wild animals" we ever saw in this valley were squirrels and stray cats. The list of interesting birds is even more fascinating; there are "squawky" black crows, mocking birds, and sparrows. Ah! Life in the city!

When we moved to our country home, one of the first stunning moments was the incredible number of stars in the heavens. I never dreamed that a person could feast on this every night. I felt like I could reach out and grab a handful of the stars. They appeared so close. The song of birds only enhanced the stillness of the days and nights. One time, a rather large flock of birds flew up from behind me, and I actually heard them before I saw them due to the sound of their wings in flight. In the warm mornings when I am out on my porch, the song of the different birds is like a chorus that fills the air with its sweetness. My children, who are all now grown and married, say that they love the smell of the country air. They will roll down their windows as they cross over our county line just to take in its fresh aroma. I don't think I have enough time to list all of the incredible animals, reptiles, and birds that share our home; they truly are wonderfully made!

1. When you woke up this morning, what was the first thing that spoke to your heart about God?

2. If you didn't notice anything, stop and ask God to reveal something special about His world.

In the Old Testament, the book of Psalms is a collection of praise and song to our God. David wrote in Psalm 19:1-6 (NLT):

> The heavens proclaim the glory of God,
> The skies display his craftsmanship.
> Day after day they continue to speak;
> night after night they make him known.
> They speak without a sound or word;
> their voice is never heard.
> Yet their message has gone throughout the earth,

and their words to all the world.
God has made a home in the heavens for the sun.
It bursts forth like a radiant bridegroom after his
wedding.
It rejoices like a great athlete eager to run the race.
The sun rises at one end of the heavens and follows its
course to the other end.
Nothing can hide from its heat.

It saddens me to think that today there are people who never get away from the city lights and congestion to take in the wonders of our Master Designer. No wonder there are so many cold and calculating hearts in our world today.

But God shows his anger from heaven against all
sinful, wicked people who suppress the truth by their
wickedness. They know the truth about God because
he has made it obvious to them. Forever since the
world was created, people have seen the earth and sky.
Through everything God made, they can clearly see his
invisible qualities—his eternal power and divine nature.
So they have no excuse for not knowing God.

Romans 1:18-20 (NLT)

In the verses above, what do they say about the wicked?

1.

2.

What are the three things we can see if we truly "look up"?

1.

2.

3.

The anger that God is expressing is the result of man's denial of the Creator. As stated in Psalm 19, God has placed the evidence for all to see and experience. The majesty in the handiworks of the Maker is not seen because of the callous heart. If we truly look intently into the creation of God, its beauty, wonder, and magnificence of design and function, a master designer cannot be ignored for the flimsy theory of happenstance.

Our skin was designed to develop these calluses as a barrier from abrasive exposure. Calluses are thick, tough, and lack sensation. Wearing gloves while working with horses is a good idea, especially around straps, reins, and ropes. You may think you have a firm grip until a 1,200-pound animal decides to pull back with all its weight. Blisters and calluses are formed when tender skin is not protected from rough and abrasive materials. This is what God means when He refers to a people who suppress the truth. They build up a callous against God because of their constant denial, and thus their hearts become calloused.

Jesus was challenging the woman at the well in the following verses. He confronted her regarding what it was that she worshiped. The Lord wanted to help her file down the calloused view of God that she had acquired.

Find a dictionary and write out the definition of "worship."

To worship means:

> "Woman," Jesus replied, "believe me, a time is coming
> when you will worship the Father neither on this
> mountain nor in Jerusalem. You Samaritans worship
> what you do not know; we worship what we do know,
> for salvation is from the Jews. Yet a time is coming and
> has now come when the true worshipers will worship
> the Father in the Spirit and in truth, for they are the
> kind of worshipers the Father seeks. God is spirit, and
> his worshipers must worship in the Spirit and in truth."
>
> John 4:21-24 (NIV)

Do you worship what you know? The truth of His being, His Spirit, His Son. The woman at the well was plugging her ears to the truth, for what she was contented with from her past. Sometimes it feels easier to go with what you know rather than lean into the truth.

So your assignment for today is to go outside and look up into the heavens! Go outside and look into the creation. Watch birds in flight, a squirrel gathering nuts, the stars in the heavens. If you live in the city, find a place to go and stare intently into the pleasure of God by admiring His creation! One of the biggest evidences of His pleasure is to look into the eyes of others. Have you noticed that as similar as we are, we are very distinct? The face of another human being is spectacular to behold. Go to a hospital nursery and gaze upon a new life that is so uniquely made. Look at your fingerprint or think about the design of your foot. God fearfully and wonderfully made everything about you!

Make a list of the things that you observed:

See what great love the Father has lavished on us, that we should be called children of God! And that is what we are! The reason the world does not know us is that it did not know him.

First John 3:1 (NIV)

Prayer:

Dear Father,

Help me to see the wonders that You have created. Help me to peel away the layers of the man-made images of this world and see to the original of Your handy work. Then, place in my heart an understanding of Your love for me. In praise of Your creation, amen.

The Acorns of this World

Day Two

We have had many horses come and go on our ranch. One particular horse, Robin, was an amazing and beautiful animal. She was the California Paint Horse state champion in her glory days. She scored her points for conformation, color, and athletic abilities. This horse had been well cared for, pampered, and had lived the life of a movie star. But as age settles in on an animal and the up-and-coming new stars arrive in the show arena, it is out with the old and in with the new. She had been retired from the show circuit to a breeding farm and was to be sold at an auction. It is a sad but common tale that due to an illness of the owner, the ranch and its assets are being liquidated.

I have a dear friend, Avery, who had undertaken the task of training my daughters how to ride, breed, and care for their horses. This auction was an incredible opportunity for my daughters, who were breeding horses for color, to acquire a good breeding mare. Avery is a very special lady who gives with all her heart to the tasks of life. So off Avery went with my two oldest girls to buy a special horse at this auction. When the bidding ended that weekend, Avery and my girls loaded our trailer with three horses and started for home. As the truck and trailer pulled into the barn area that night, we were all so excited as this majestic animal was unloaded from the trailer. Robin was tall and well built, sorrel with white and two blue-violet eyes lined with black. She was stunning and, best of all, pregnant with a very promising foal!

After the usual time of adjusting to her new location and getting to know the other horses in the herd, it was time to let her out to pasture. It is always a thrill to see an animal released onto open spaces. The horses will run with their necks arched, nostrils flared (taking in all the scents of their new home), tails up, and occasionally, a little buck is kicked up in approval.

After a couple of days of adjusting to the new pasture, we noticed that she was up on a hill, eating under an old oak tree. She didn't congregate with the other horses. She stayed up there and ate and ate. This was an unusual pattern for a horse. So up my daughter went with halter in hand to bring this mare back down to the barn. What this horse was up to was gorging on acorns. She had never had the opportunity to eat as much of whatever she wanted. Having come from the "show circuit," she had lived a very regimented life. She had eaten herself sick on acorns!

Acorns are loaded with tannic acid, which, when eaten in large amounts, can kill a horse. She became so ill that a bad colic followed, and vet care included an IV to get emergency fluids into her system. Colic is a condition in which there is a sudden onset of abdominal pain. It can be caused by spasms, inflammation, or an obstruction. In horses, it is very serious and usually fatal.

Here is the beginning of the problem of those who are empty. They are on a constant search to fill up with anything that might make the meaninglessness fade away. Some try to fill up on success. For others, it may be the numbing effects of drugs or alcohol.

Money can give a false sense of power that can drive a person to hunger for more and more. Or how about the prestige of education? Anything we can stuff into our vacant lives to make that gnawing empty sensation disappear. Until we fill up on the living water, we will always only know satisfaction for a short season. And when we fill up on what the world has to offer and not God, there are consequences like colic in our lives.

Read Ephesians 2:1-6 in your Bible. Take a moment to be still and listen to the Lord, then read again before we move forward in today's lesson. Now I would like to take a walk with you through these verses as described in the Message.

> It wasn't so long ago that you were mired in that old stagnant life of sin. You let the world, which doesn't know the first thing about living, tell you how to live. You filled your lungs with polluted unbelief, and then exhaled disobedience. We all did it, all of us doing what we felt like doing, when we felt like doing it, all of us in the same boat. It's a wonder God didn't lose his temper and do away with the whole lot of us. Instead, immense in mercy and with an incredible love, he embraced us. He took our sin-dead lives and made us alive in Christ. He did all this on his own, with no help from us! Then he picked us up and set us down in highest heaven in company with Jesus, our Messiah.
>
> Ephesians 2:1-6 (MSG)

"Stagnant" is defined as "not flowing or moving, lack of motion, not developing or making progress, not active or lively." "To be mired in something" means "to be caught up, hindered, held up, or stuck."

Can you remember what it was like? Or maybe you are not quite sure if you ever left what the world had to offer. That type of lifestyle that is stale, impure, or inferior. The life of not moving forward and feasting on what the world has to offer is not the life that God designed you for. The use of the word "world" is used to describe the things that are temporal. Here for the moment. Not things of eternal value.

Place an X on the line below to indicate where you think you are relative to God versus the world.

l_____l

THE WORLD   GOD

1.Describe where you think you are in the world or with God.

Jesus answered her, "If you knew the gift of God and who it is that asks you for a drink, you would have asked him and he would have given you living water."

John 4:10 (NIV)

"Jesus said, 'Everyone who drinks this water will get thirsty again and again. Anyone who drinks the water I give will never thirst—not ever. The water I give will be an artesian spring within, gushing fountains of endless life."

John 4:13-14, (MSG)

Jesus has and is the living water, not polluted and free for the asking. Why do people search from one quest to another, trying frantically to fill the heart-shaped vacuum that only God's love can satisfy? I would venture to say that they have tasted the "acorns of life" that sicken but produce powerful feelings of physical desire for more and more. Until we, as God's created, get the IV solution of living water, we will always thirst. You see, intravenous fluids go directly into our blood to repair the damage that a lack of hydration has caused. Like the lonely woman at the well, who day after day returns to drink from the world, she is actually empty of the water that satisfies. She is burdened with the things of this world that hinder her from moving into the fulfilled life.

She has filled her jar with the things of the world that suppress the truth of the living God. She has filled her jar with the polluted waters that hinder.

In the above verses from Ephesians 2:1-6 and John 4:10, 13-14, place the words in the column that either describes the world or God.

THE WORLD   GOD

Prayer:

Dear Father God,

 I either am or know of someone who thirsts after the things of this world, not You and Your gift of eternal life. Please, Father, as I continue on this road of discovery, open my eyes that I might see, my ears to hear, my mind to understand, and my heart to receive the living water of eternal life for myself. I also lift up to You those in my life who do not know You, that they too will begin to understand and thirst no more. I pray this in the name of Jesus, the Savior of the world, amen.

Are You Empty?

Day Three

Habits are the things that we do without thinking yet produce a desired result. Horses can become very habitual in their daily routines, especially when it comes to something that they want and want now! When the water troughs in the horse pasture become empty, one of our horses, a bay mare named Star, bangs her hoof on the sidewall of the trough. Knock, knock, knock would come echoing from the trough. It is a great alert system that lets us know that the water trough needs filling. An important alert system at that! Star is our lead or "boss mare," keeper of the herd. She is first in everything, whether yielded or demanded. Sometimes when you walk down to the horse pasture, she turns her rump to you. This is your signal that she is dissatisfied with the service at the ranch. The routine for us is to place the hose into the trough, turn on the faucet and begin to fill the empty container. Star will occasionally look over her shoulder and down her rump at you to check your work. Once content that you are doing an adequate job, she will turn around, give a nip to any other horse standing too close and wait. Wait for what you may ask? For you to move ever so slightly away from the hose, and then bam! She will grab the hose and fling it up in the air to get you wet. Her way of saying, "Next time, don't let it get empty."

Empty, drained, not containing anything, without meaning or purpose, devoid of vitality. Can you relate to any of these descriptions? Empty can also refer to a feeling or a "state of being." Like the water trough, we can be empty as human beings. Our existence without a soul that is satisfied can be very vacant. Do you ever feel empty or devoid of God? An empty existence is a very dry trough waiting to be filled.

1. Are you full or empty? Please describe.

2. Do you know someone who is empty?

3. Can you share a time that you felt filled up with God's love?

Before I became a Christian, I had this sense that there was an empty space in my life. I felt that life had more to offer than my understanding of it. Even at the tender age of ten, I knew that the love I received from my family was conditional and not complete; I had to earn it. The love I received from my parents by "being good" had strings attached. The problem was that I was not perfect, so the love was not dependable. And because I did not understand who the Lord was, I was empty of God's love.

So who are the empty? The empty are those who do not have a personal relationship with God or have walked away from Him. It may be you or someone that you know. The love of God is something they or you have not experienced or have denied because of some bad habits.

> Do not love the world or anything in the world. If anyone loves the world, love for the Father is not in them. For everything in the world—the lust of the flesh, the lust of the eyes, and the pride of life—comes not from the Father but from the world. The world and its desires pass away, but whoever does the will of God lives forever.
>
> First John 2:15-17 (NIV)

1. What are the three things in the verses above that are not from God?

2. Can you, as a Christian or non-Christian, identify any love of the world in your heart or mind?

3. What does doing the will of God do for us?

4. But whoever does the will of God _____ forever.

5. Do you want to live with God forever?

So we are told not to love the world or anything in it. We should not set our sights on this world and what is in it. As believers in Jesus, rather we are to "look up" to our heavenly home. Our goal and focus are to be heaven-bound.

Please reread verses 4-9 (NIV) from the woman at the well:

> Now he had to go through Samaria. So he came to a town in Samaria called Sychar, near the plot of ground Jacob had given to his son Joseph. Jacob's well was there, and Jesus, tired as he was from the journey, sat down by the well. It was about noon. When a Samaritan woman came to draw water, Jesus said to her, "Will you give me a drink?" (His disciples had gone into the town to buy food.) The Samaritan woman said to him, "You are a Jew and I am a Samaritan woman. How can you ask me for a drink?" (For Jews do not associate with Samaritans.) Jesus answered her, "If you knew the gift of God and who it is that asks you for a drink, you would have asked him and he would have given you living water."

6. Do you know what gift God wants to give?

> For you know that God paid a ransom to save you from
> the empty life you inherited from your ancestors. And
> the ransom he paid was not mere gold or silver. It was
> the precious blood of Christ, the sinless, spotless Lamb
> of God. God chose him as your ransom long before the
> world began, but he has now revealed him to you in
> these last days. Through Christ you have come to trust
> in God. And you have placed your faith and hope in
> God because he raised Christ from the dead and gave
> him great glory.
>
> First Peter 1:18-21 (NLT)

To have our ransom paid suggests that we needed to be
freed from a hazardous situation. This verse states that we were
ransomed from a life without meaning. That is pretty powerful, to
be freed from an empty life, an existence devoid of God. Having
no longer to remain in the dried-up world, we are filled instead
with the living water of God!

> On the last day, the climax of the festival, Jesus stood
> and shouted to the crowds, 'Anyone who is thirsty may
> come to me! Anyone who believes in me may come and
> drink! For the Scriptures declare, "Rivers of living water
> will flow from his heart."
>
> John 7:37-38 (NLT)

Fill in the blanks:

If you _____, you can come and drink.

Then, living waters will flow from His _____.

Have you received the free gift? If not, what is holding you back?

Prayer:

Dear Lord,

Help me to identify my need for the "living water." I want to fill up on You and You alone. Empty is not where I want to be. Thank You for Your living water that can quench my deepest thirst.

Or maybe your prayer is praise:

Praise:

Lord, thank You for filling me up! You took my dried-up soul and filled it with Your love. In Jesus' sweet name, amen.

Or maybe your prayer is a request:

My request:

Dear Lord,

Will You please be with _____? They are empty
and need Your free gift; help them to come to You for the living
waters. Thank You, Lord, for hearing my prayer. Amen.

Or maybe you need a "restart":

My restart:

Dear Father,

I confess that the emptiness I am feeling is my doing. Lord,
please forgive me for trusting the world rather than You. I need
a fresh start. Please help me to trust You and You alone to fill me
up. Thank You, merciful Father. Amen.

THIRSTY

WEEK TWO

The Manure Pile

Day Four

As time passed and foaling season drew near, my husband's business required him to be away from home for some very long days and even some overnight trips. With five children, homeschooling, church activities, 4-H, and other daily reminders that I was in over my head with chores and responsibilities, I was looking for some shortcuts to my chores.

Pregnant mares are usually provided a wonderfully clean stall with a good depth of straw for a safe delivery. The problem is that you don't know when they are going to deliver, and we had three mares ready to foal at the same time. The girls would go in every morning, clean out all the soiled straw while the mare was out in the paddock. Then in the evening, the mare would get all prepped in case her time was near. My daughters slept in the barn to keep a close watch on the mares that January for four weeks in anticipation of the foals' births.

Four weeks equals a lot of straw and manure piling up around the ranch. As the pile got bigger and bigger, I wanted to rid myself of the piles sooner than later. That is when I had what I thought was a great solution to my dilemma. If I could just light that pile on fire, it would be gone in no time. Not taking the precaution to ask anyone if this was a good idea or not, I proceeded with my plan. I knew deep in my heart that I should not lean on my own understanding of how to burn a pile of debris, a manure-and-urine-soaked, damp pile of icky straw. Well, needless to say that my bad judgment was obvious to anyone within a few ranches from us. It was the biggest, most awful, green smoke bomb I have ever seen! Oh, how our sins will find us out!

What is sin? Sin is the expression of selfish actions and thoughts that we put before God. Anytime I put a priority on myself or something else before God, I sin. For example, the manure pile. I wanted a quick fix. I knew in my heart that if I called my husband, he would have told me not to light the pile on fire. But a nagging voice in my ear said, "You don't have the time to deal with all these chores. All you have to do is light that pile on fire, and poof, it will be out of the way." As I am about to light the pile, I hear another still small voice suggest that "You should call a friend and find out if this is a safe and good idea." I light it anyway because "I deserve a break from all of my many chores. After all, I had a hard day today, and nobody will know." This is a good example of putting what I wanted before what God wants. He would have me look for the right way of doing things rather than the shortcuts. God would want me to humble myself and ask someone who knows better. God would have had me talk with my husband, not avoid a conversation that I knew would not go my way.

By lighting that horrible pile on fire, I put the "I" in sIn.

> So whether you eat or drink or whatever you do, do it all for the glory of God. Do not cause anyone to stumble, whether Jews, Greeks or the church of God— even as I try to please everyone in every way. For I am not seeking my own good but the good of many, so that they may be saved.
>
> First Corinthians 10:31-33 (NIV)

"I" before God equals sIn.

Sin destroys.

Sin falls short of making the goal.

Sin is separation from God forever.

Sin is death without the Savior.

Sin is darkness.

In your columns from day two, you should have:

THE WORLD

sin, dead lives, stagnant, disobedience, mired, and thirsty.

GOD

love, eternal life, living water, never thirst, gift of God, alive in Christ, heaven, and Jesus.

> For the wages which sin pays is death, but the [bountiful] free gift of God is eternal life through (in union with) Jesus Christ our Lord.
>
> Romans 6:23 (AMP)

The term "wages" means that you earned it, so sin earns the reimbursement of death. This "death" is an unending separation from God. In other words, to live in hell is to live forever without God. And heaven (Oh, what an amazing place! A topic for another study.) is to live forever with God.

> For everyone has sinned; we all fall short of God's glorious standard.
>
> Romans 3:23 (NLT)

To "fall short" means you didn't make it. Did you get that? Oh, hello! It says "everyone," not just a few of the really naughty people from this world. It is like running a horse race and stopping before the finish line. You could be an eighth of a mile or two inches from the finish line; if you don't cross the line, you didn't finish the race.

> He saved us, not because of righteous things we had done, but because of his mercy. He saved us through the washing of rebirth and renewal by the Holy Spirit.
>
> Titus 3:55 (NIV)

Get out your dictionary and look up the definition of "mercy" and write it in the space below:

> God saved you by his grace when you believed. And you can't take credit for this; it is a gift from God. Salvation is not a reward for the good things we have done, so none of us can boast about it.
>
> Ephesians 2:8-9 (NLT)

Now, look up "grace" and write down it's definition below:

For God so greatly loved and dearly prized the world
that He [even] gave up His only begotten [unique] Son,
so that whoever believes in [trusts in, clings to, relies
on] Him shall not perish [come to destruction, be lost]
but have eternal [everlasting] life.

John 3:16 (AMP)

I want to really look deep into the well of truth, so I am
giving you several ways to look at what is being said in the Bible.
This is from the Message.

This is how much God loved the world: He gave his
Son, his one and only Son. And this is why: so that no
one need be destroyed; by believing in him, anyone can
have a whole and lasting life. God didn't go to all the
trouble of sending his Son merely to point an accusing
finger, telling the world how bad it was. He came to
help, to put the world right again. Anyone who trusts
in him is acquitted; anyone who refuses to trust him
has long since been under the death sentence without
knowing it. And why? Because of that person's failure
to believe in the one-of-a-kind Son of God when
introduced to him.

John 3:16-18 (MSG)

God showed his love for us when he sent his only Son
into the world to give us life. Real love isn't our love
for God, but his love for us. God sent his Son to be the
sacrifice by which our sins are forgiven.

First John 4:9-10 (CEV)

So we have learned what the worldly mindset is full of, the
pride of life, the lust of the flesh and the eyes. But this reference

to the world is referring to the entire creation; God's pleasure is in his people of the earth. There is no need to be separated from God; no pointing fingers here! We are given the opportunity to live a whole and lasting life.

> If you declare with your mouth, "Jesus is Lord," and believe in your heart that God raised him from the dead, you will be saved. For it is with your heart that you believe and are justified, and it is with your mouth that you profess your faith and are saved.
>
> Romans 10:9-10 (NIV)

This is where our faith or belief takes action by us sharing with others. We have gone from not understanding to knowledge. We have gone from knowing to telling others about the love of God for us. Mercy is not receiving what we really ought to take delivery of. In other words, you really deserve to have it, but the "just judge" says, "Not guilty"! You are forgiven!

Grace is unmerited favor. Favor is something that you didn't earn. To favor something is to show approval.

God is love.

God is absolute.

God gives grace and mercy.

God is eternal, forever and ever, timeless in time.

God is God.

He believes in you, His creation, regardless of your belief in Him!

"For everyone who asks, receives. Everyone who seeks, finds. And to everyone who knocks, the door will be opened."

Luke 11:10 (NIV)

Remember the "knock, knock, knock" of the empty trough earlier this week? God is knocking at the door of your heart. Will you listen and answer? Will you fill up with the living water?

Do you, as a Christian/non-Christian, have a stinky manure pile that needs to be taken care of? It is either time for a new beginning or a time to clean up the things that stink.

Believe... Declare... Be saved!

Prayer

Dear Lord,

I understand that I have fallen short and have sinned. You created me to be loved by You and to love You. I know how to receive this eternal love by declaring that You gave the world Your Son Jesus. I believe that He died on the cross for my sins and rose from the dead, so I could be saved forever and ever to live with You. Please forgive me for putting me first. Thank You for the free gift of salvation, for loving me so very much, and for saving me, a sinner. In Jesus' precious and powerful name, amen!

Upward, Inward, and Outward
Day Five

God wants to connect with us just like He wanted to connect with the woman at the well when He asked her, "Will you give me a drink?" Remember that this would have required contact to be made. He arranged this meeting so that they could have time away from others. Jesus wants us to be part of His plan, the plan that you and I should live eternally with Him, not without Him. Are you part of this plan?

When we were starting out with the horses, Avery introduced us to the world of 4-H. It provided us with the information about the "horse community" that we needed. There was a pledge, a handbook, membership fees, and of course, the white and green uniform. I asked one of my daughters the other day if she remembered her pledge; she was able to, on the spot, recite that pledge. It meant something to her; she desired a place in that group. 4-H was a kind of a family.

We, too, as believers, are part of the family of God. We need to connect with God and never forget our pledge...the acceptance of His Son Jesus as our Savior. As members of our new family, we can refer to a sort of handbook for solutions to the things that we don't understand. Our handbook, the Bible, is more like a manual of operations. If we follow the instructions on how to be a good member, things will go well with us. So the first step is to read it. I know we can all relate to a time we thought we did not need to go to the instructions to see how to get something up and running. Only to find that cutting corners only produced its own set of consequences. Following the directions yields the end product as it was designed to be. Membership fees are not literally paid in this family, but they are still felt in one way or another. A great example is the woman at the well. She had opted not to marry male partner number six. Thus, isolation from the other women in the village, loneliness, and scorn were part of her daily existence.

The next picture story that I would like to draw our attention to is the white and Kelly green uniform. If you have ever been to a county or state fair, you have seen the uniforms of those kids as they proudly exhibit their projects. The uniform is evidence of the commitment of their project of the year and the "family" in which they belong. We, too, are to show public testimony to the commitment we have made to the family of Christ, our Redeemer, by...

UPWARD

We look up to the heavens to God's creation. We are acknowledging God as Creator.

INWARD

We believe, receive, and declare the gift of God into our hearts. His love now resides in us.

OUTWARD

We publicly display our connection with God by baptism and showing the love we received from Jesus flowing out of our hearts.

Now, I don't want to rub anyone's coat the wrong way, and I will state this up front. I am not saying that it is what is on the outside of a person that counts, far from it! We need to be looking up to the Master, processing it on the inside so we can pour it out as evidence of the change on the inside.

Upward, inward, and outward!

It is time to go to our instruction manual to see what I am rambling on about today. Remember, in the beginning of John chapter 4, Jesus was with John as he was baptizing new believers.

So what is baptism and its importance?

> Well then, should we keep on sinning so that God can show us more and more of his wonderful grace? Of course not! Since we have died to sin, how can we continue to live in it? Or have you forgotten that when we were joined with Christ Jesus in baptism, we joined him in his death? For we died and were buried with Christ by baptism. And just as Christ was raised from the dead by the glorious power of the Father, now we also may live new lives.
>
> Romans 6:1-4 (NIV)

> Since we have been united with him in his death, we will also be raised to life as he was. We know that our old sinful selves were crucified with Christ so that sin might lose its power in our lives. We are no longer slaves to sin. For when we died with Christ we were set free from the power of sin. And since we died with Christ, we know we will also live with him. We are sure of this because Christ was raised from the dead, and he will never die again. Death no longer has any power over him. When he died, he died once to break the power of sin. But now that he lives, he lives for the glory of God.
>
> Romans 6:5-10 (NLT)

Name three things that the above verses tell us about who we now are in Christ.

1.

2.

3.

In the early church, a commitment to Jesus and baptism usually followed closely together. Today, in most Christian circles, a baptism celebration is a scheduled time of public testimony. It is an outward witness to the inside change. We are saying to the world that we have become part of a new family. Let me put it this way:

1. A profession, declaration of your new belief. You are not afraid to identify yourself with Jesus as Savior.

2. A statement of your faith, that your "old self," the part that identified itself with the "acorns of life," is dead. Thus, into the water you are submerged to signify burial of the old self.

3. A new life, up from the water you come, risen in the new life with your Lord; it is like you just buried the old person, and now you start all over again. It is like a birthday party, the celebration of your new life. When you have connected to this new life, you will gladly wear the new uniform of the new self!

Matthew 28:16-20 is known as the "Great Commission." Read this section of verses in your own Bible.

Jesus is giving testimony to His disciples that they are to go out into the world to teach others what He has told them and to baptize in the name (this is who has the power and authority) of the Father, Son, and Holy Spirit. By doing this, they will increase the number of disciples or followers. And I love the last verse; He, Jesus, will always be with us!

Now, look up Acts 2:36-41.

In verse 38, Peter gives the questioning people some instructions. He tells the people to _____ and be _____.

In Isaiah 44, the Lord is speaking to those He created, and He states in verse 3-4 (NIV):

> For I will pour water on the thirsty land, and streams on the dry ground; I will pour out my Spirit on your offspring, and my blessing on your descendants. They will spring up like grass in a meadow, like poplar trees by flowing streams.

What a beautiful picture story of the poplar tree sending down its roots to drink from the streams and God pouring out His blessing.

Again, further on in Romans 8:1-17, Paul gives a very powerful testimony to the Holy Spirit. Read it, then fill in the blanks.

Verse 1-3: God sent His _____ to end the control that _____ has over us.

Verse 4-5: If the Spirit controls you, you will think about things that _____ God.

Verse 7-8: Those controlled by their sinful nature _____ please God.

Verse 10-11: Your _____ will die because of sin, but because the Spirit of _____ lives in you, He will give you _____ life.

Rewrite verses 12-17 in your own words.

See how great a love the Father has bestowed on us,
that we would be called children of God; and such we
are For this reason the world does not know us, because
it did not know Him.

First John 3:1 (NASB)

If you have questions regarding baptism, please see your
pastor or your small group leader for more information.

Prayer:

Thank You, Lord, for bringing me into Your family. For loving
me so much that You have very carefully made provisions for me
to be included in Your plans. Lord, I lift up to You those on my
list that need to come into Your family. Will You please stir their
hearts to receive Your living waters? In Jesus' name, amen.

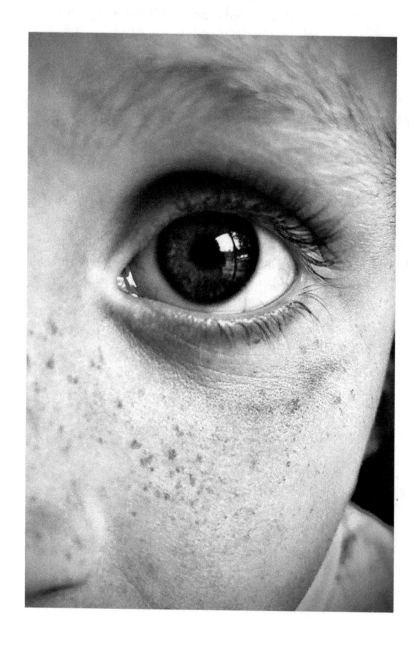

WEEK THREE

How Do You *Know* That...You Know God?

What you know in this life helps to shape who you become in this timeframe of "peoplehood." Where you spend your time molds what you learn. What you have learned manifests as action and intention. To know something takes time and experience; you were not born knowing; you were just gifted with a brain. God created us to use that gift for His glory and purpose, but He loves us so much that He gave us freedom in thought. This freedom is a wild card in our lives and can take us places where sometimes we wonder how we got there. When all the dust settles, will you be sitting all alone by a well with a heart full of regret? Or will you know that you know God and His love?

What Do You Know?

Day One

If you know your horse, you will know its needs. This is
a simple statement for a simple solution, a solution for many
of the problems in the horse world. By knowing my animal, I
know what it requires and how to satisfy that need. If my horse's
needs are met and satisfied, it then wants to please me. We have
successfully built a relationship of trust that connects us by the
care provided.

One of the things that Avery taught my girls was how to take
good care of their animals. My girls loved Avery and knew that
she was very wise in the horse kingdom. She taught them to love
their animals by providing for their needs. The week before we
brought one of our first horses to our ranch, she had the girls
prepping its new home. The girls put on their work clothes and
went to work. Our ranch was an old sheep ranch that had to be
converted to accommodate a taller and stronger animal. The
fences had to have an additional wire added; the gates needed
to be upgraded to something stronger, taller, and wider. In the
barn, they took their hammers and hit down all the nails that had
pried up over the years. They covered the dirt with sawdust to
absorb smells and urine. New light bulbs replaced old ones, and
of course, the troughs had to be scrubbed, disinfected, then filled
with clean drinking water. This was a labor of love for two very
eager young girls. These girls had to abandon a time of leisurely
play for commitment. They were determined to show their love

to these horses, to earn Avery's approval and the trust of the horses as they cared for them.

This last one is very important. If the horses know that you are there to provide for them, they begin to trust you. With trust, they develop a desire to take risks for you. For example, have you ever thought about why an animal that was designed with the instinct called "fight or flight" would possibly want to load into a "giant tin can" called a horse trailer? It makes noises when they step onto the unstable footing. When loaded, there is no place to run from danger. Then, to make matters worst, that same "tin can" moves! Not only on familiar ground but down a highway with loud vehicles with horns and motors. And then, here is the kicker; a well-trained and trusting horse will load back up after it has gotten out onto solid ground. Why? Because they trust and know that the person in charge cares for their safety and has their best interest at heart.

You see, it takes time to train a horse to do this astounding behavior of loading into a horse trailer. Care, love, patience, discipline, repetition, the list goes on and on. The bottom line is that a relationship has been established upon getting familiar with the animal; thus, the animal trusts in its owner. It is worthy of mentioning that I will not load a horse I don't trust! I want to know the animal I am getting into a "tin can" without a place for me to run! I have learned that the hard way; accidents happen. If I do not know the animal and what triggers that "fight or flight" reaction, I do not go in a trailer with it.

Look up the definition for "know" and write it down:

I want you to take a few minutes or a day if needed to truly contemplate this question. Say it out loud to yourself, hear yourself ask the question. It will help you to discern the inflection of the question if you say it out loud. Meditate on it, examine your heart, search your understanding of God, and then answer the best you can before we look further into the inquiry. So let me ask you a very important question...

How do you know... that...you know God?

When ready, write out your response in the space below.

In this following text, Paul is speaking to the new believers in Philippi. He wants them to grab onto the idea of knowledge based upon experience, not intellectual facts.

> I once thought these things were valuable, but now I consider them worthless because of what Christ has done. Yes, everything else is worthless when compared with the infinite value of knowing Christ Jesus my Lord. For his sake I have discarded everything else, counting it all as garbage, so that I could gain Christ and become one with him. I no longer count on my own righteousness through obeying the law; rather, I become righteous through faith in Christ. For God's way of making us right with himself depends on faith. I want to know Christ and experience the mighty power that raised him from the dead. I want to suffer with him, sharing in his death, so that one way or another I will experience the resurrection from the dead!
>
> Philippians 3:7-11 (NLT)

In Philippians, it is Paul who is speaking to us. Who was Paul? Look up in your Bible Philippians 3:4-6. Paul states in those verses that he had placed his confidence of who he was in what he was. He gives his list of credentials of the who's who of the religious community of his time. He continues on in the verses that followed to explain that the law had no more hold or power over him because of what Jesus did for him. Then, in verse 10, he explains that to know Christ is to experience His mighty power. What a mental overhaul Paul had to go through. He no longer could earn righteousness by following the law. Think of all those years of trying to be right before God; they were all a waste compared to knowing and experiencing the power of the resurrection.

1. What have you experienced about the mighty power of God?

> After Jesus said these things, he looked toward heaven
> and prayed, "Father, the time has come. Give glory to
> your Son so that the Son can give glory to you. You gave
> the Son power over all people so that the Son could give
> eternal life to all those you gave him. And this is eternal
> life: that people know you, the only true God, and that
> they know Jesus Christ, the One you sent."
>
> John 17:1-3 (NCV)

"That they know you" to believe and firmly understand the
truth about God. "The only true God," the genuine and actual
God, creator of all things. "Jesus Christ," the Son of God sent
to ransom us from death. Death is the "forever" separation
from God. Jesus paid the price of our falling short of perfection
and holiness. To know God takes time spent learning through
experience and study. We need to look at all the aspects of what
God has to offer us. We need to take a hold of His truth, His
absolute truth. That He is God, and we are in need of God to love
us and take care of us.

1. How can we guard ourselves from creating God into something that He is not?

2. Share a time that you witnessed God's provision in a time of need.

3. List the truth that you know about God's

    a. love

    b. word

    c. justice

    d. boundaries

    e. provision

In order to know God as God is, you must guard yourselves from recreating Him into something that He is not so that you will know that you know God. Do you want to know Christ? Then, hold onto your saddle horn for the ride of your life!

Prayer:

Dear Lord,

I want to know You. I want to truly know You. Please, help me to erase the things that are not true about You in my understanding of You. Any wrong thoughts or concepts that I have applied to who You are in my life, please replace with the truth. I want to know with confidence that I know You. In the power of the cross, amen.

"For My thoughts are not your thoughts, nor are your ways My ways," declares the LORD. "For as the heavens are higher than the earth, so are My ways higher than your ways And My thoughts than your thoughts."

Isaiah 55:8-9 (NASB)

THIRSTY

Imprinted with His Love

Day Two

It was always exciting when a new foal was born on the ranch. A foal would become the focus of our time, thought, and energy. We would want to get to know that foal and the foal to get to know us. Through contact, we experienced each other, and thus, our knowledge of one another increased.

In our foaling stall, we would do what we call "imprinting." Imprinting is the process of bonding a newborn foal not only to its mother but also to us as an important part of its life. It facilitates and shapes lifetime behavior for the horse. This is a very sweet time in the early hours of a new life. The technique that we use is to approach the mare, and then, when she is comfortable with us being there, we begin to handle the foal. First, we will breathe gently into the nostrils allowing the foal to imprint our scent. Next, we begin to speak softly to the foal like the mare who sweetly knickers to her precious baby. Then, ever so tenderly, we will run our hands all over the foal, inside the ears, mouth, under the belly; we even will pick up their hooves and tap gently. All of these movements signal to this horse that it is okay to be handled by a human. We try to do this on a daily basis; each day reaffirms who we are. This increases the foal's knowledge by positive experience that we are an important part of the "herd." This intimate connection and experience allow us to increase our knowledge of one another. Have you noticed that Jesus makes contact to imprint upon the women at the well a positive experience with Him?

What positive experience have you had with another believer?

> A woman of Samaria came to draw water. Jesus said to her, "Give Me a drink."
>
> John 4:7 (NKJV)

Explain what you think Jesus was doing to imprint a positive experience with the woman at the well.

We touched this subject back in week one, regarding the separation of the Jews from the Samaritans. Jesus, by asking the woman for a drink, was, in essence, saying, "I don't care what tradition says about the relationships we should have. Instead, I am going to break through those barriers of relationship and act according to the love that My Father in heaven has imprinted on My heart for you and the world."

She is a Samaritan, a woman, and an outcast from her community. But Jesus is saying that, according to God's economy, she is whom He came to save from the wickedness of this world. Jesus gives us hope for a better tomorrow, and He pours into us His amazing love.

Imprinting does a marvelous thing for a young foal's life; it impresses positive behavior as a result of a good experience. But what about the old gray mares and bucking broncos of life that over time have become what they call barn sour? Unfortunately, they have been conditioned to exhibit bad behavior as a defense to unpleasant handling.

Sacking out is a method of retraining a horse to accept the scary things in its life. You expose the horse to the item of fear very carefully and a little at a time until it is no longer associated with something terrible. You are essentially desensitizing a horse to a potentially frightening situation or object. Some of these occurrences may have been induced by an inexperienced or a cruel handler, or sometimes, at the most inopportune moment, equipment can fail, causing things to go wrong fast. I once tied my horse to its usual hitching post when something startled him. With a sudden jerk and all of the animal's strength, he pulled up and back. This caused a malfunction in the safety snap, and to make matters worse, my slipknot failed. As the horse continued to pull, this yanked the entire hitching post up and out of the ground. Talk about a situation taking a turn for the worst! That horse, needless to say, panicked and ran around our property dragging a fence post until he was utterly exhausted. It took a lot of careful sacking out to get that horse to tie up to a hitching post again.

Were your early imprints good ones? Mine were not. I knew love was there, but the imprinting was not done correctly. So I needed some sacking out by our Master Trainer. How about you? Do you need to have some of the world's imprints erased and replaced by God's love? Make a list of some of the imprints that need to be replaced in your life by the Master Trainer.

My lists of items to be "sacked out" of my life are as follows:

I would like to have the "Master Trainer" replace them with His imprinting. This is a list of the imprinting that I need:

So how does God retrain us to trust in Him?

> This is my prayer for you: that your love will grow more and more; that you will have knowledge and understanding with your love.
>
> Philippians 1:9 (NCV)

Read 1 Corinthians 13:1-7. In verses 1-3, What does Paul say that without _____ we are like a resounding gong or a clanging cymbal? Now I have to admit that I have met some resounding gongs in my life! It is like they are all prickly without love.

In verses 4-7, the Bible lists what love is and is not. Write down the list:

LOVE IS   LOVE IS NOT

So what does the overflowing love of God look like? In the beginning of verse 8, in 1 Corinthians 13, it says that love never fails. Why? Because this is the type of love that comes from God. Notice the difference between your two lists. The "love is" list does not require a lovable beneficiary. This love comes from the deep wells of "living waters." Our roots have dug down deep, just like the poplar tree in Isaiah 44:3-4, to receive His love. The roots search for the truth in the Bible, the instructions from the Word of God. On the other hand, the "love is not" list is the way we used to love when we put the desires of self (sIn) first before God.

I want you to read Proverbs chapter 3, but first, look at verses 1-3. The Proverbs give instructions as a father would to his son. It tells us not to forget the father's teaching, to follow his commands that are a result of his thorough knowledge of

God. This father knows God and His way. Now, finish the third chapter of Proverbs, and I want you to pray for God to "sack you out" with His love and truth. As you reread the chapter, let Him imprint on you five points that you need to impress upon your heart.

My five points are as follows:

1.

2.

3.

4.

5.

The "what you need to do" are followed by an "I will" of promise by God. So what are the "I will do" of the above five points that you selected? For example, if I trust in the Lord, He will make my path straight.

1.

2.

3.

4.

5.

God wants to "sack out" the things in our life that hinder us from being what He designed us to be. I want you to take some quiet time with the Lord and allow Him to speak the truth of His word to your heart. For some, it may be reading His Word; for others, it might be through His creation. Whatever it is, He loves it when we look to Him for the fingerprints of His love to be impressed upon our hearts for His glory!

Prayer:

Dear sweet Lord,

Thank You for Your love. Thank You for taking the time to patiently impress me with the truth of Your love. Please open my ears to hear the truth of this love so I can come closer and closer to the child of God that You created me to be. In His grace and love, amen.

Write what it is that you hear God saying:

little "g"... BIG "G"...

Day Three

So how do you know that you know God? I mean, really know God. My husband and I were having one of those conversations about looking deep into the well of "living water." I was very perplexed about a situation in my ministry. And I was expressing to him that someone I knew only had a "god" with a little "g" that was like a genie in a bottle. Every time they got into trouble, they would rub their "magic bottle," and out came their "little god" to answer their cry. This is not the God of the Bible. But wait...there is a part of that explanation of who they thought God was that is true. Our God does care about us. This is a true part of God. In the book of Nahum, it says:

> The LORD is good, a refuge in times of trouble. He cares for those who trust in him.
>
> Nahum 1:7, (NIV)

Remember yesterday we discovered in Proverbs 3 that we need to follow His plan, then things will go right with us. So back to my question: Do you really know God for who He is according to the Bible and your personal relationship that has yielded fruit? Or do you know (create a god to fit your needs) only what you want to see? Do you design a little "g" god to fit your desires? A little "g" god that is convenient. Look again at that verse; this is His character based upon our actions. Let me state it this way. Because I trust that God is God (not me, not anything or anybody else) and that He is what He says He is, He then will take care of my needs. In the book of Nahum, the problem was that Nineveh didn't trust or honor the Lord. They did horrible things that angered God and were just about to be wiped out. The point is that even when things may not make sense, those who trust in God will be taken care of because they seek comfort and shelter from God; they take refuge.

Here is another one where our action generates a God response. He says if we do what He says, He then brings into being what He promised. Look up Matthew 5:6.

If we _____, then we will be _____.

Do you know only a little "god"? Or do you know and thirst for the God of the Bible? Now, here I go again, but this needs to be said: Do you know the God of the entire Bible?

Remember in week one, we talked about seeing the whole horse before purchasing it. Well, guess what? You need to know the God you serve by doing a couple of things. Let's go to the book of James chapter 4 for the remainder of the day. Look up in your own Bible James 4:1-11. Read it, then ask God to open your eyes to see what He wants you to see, to have the strength to change your heart and attitudes. Remember that in the book of James, the instructions are being given to the believers.

Okay, are you ready?

In verses 1-3, what are the things that James 4 says we are doing that are not right? List the five items.

1.

2.

3.

4.

5.

Why don't you get what you want? Here is a hint, look at verse 1.

What should you do?

Verse 4 says if you are _____ to the world, you are
_____ to God.

Verse 5 says that God is jealous and protective of the _____
that He has given us. In other words, take care of the gift given to
us in the Holy Spirit.

Verse 6, "God opposes the _____ but shows favor to the
_____."

Paul continues to say that He gives us more grace or greater
kindness, and that is why we should respond or act accordingly by
doing the following in verses 7-10. I like the following translation:

> Surrender to God! Resist the devil, and he will run from
> you. Come near to God, and he will come near to you.
> Clean up your lives, you sinners. Purify your hearts, you
> people who can't make up your mind. Be sad and sorry
> and weep. Stop laughing and start crying. Be gloomy
> instead of glad. Be humble in the Lord's presence, and
> he will honor you.
>
> James 4:7-10 (CEV)

List the ten things that we are to do:

1.

2.

3.

4.

5.

6.

7.

8.

9.

10.

1. Submitting is the same as surrendering, accepting, or yielding. These are not very popular verbs in our culture today. Try this way of looking at it, "I will rearrange my way of thinking that I am number one in this world to the truth that God is God and I am not."

2. Resist, stand firm, fight back, oppose, position against, defend against, and refuse to give in to...defy the devil! And here is the victory, he will run...not walk but run, scurry, scamper, rush, run, oh run away, you devil. I am a child of the King!

3. Now, this is the type of mathematics I like. If I come near to God, He will come near to me. This is where I should have been in the first place. What if we strived to stay near to God? Do you think that life might be a whole lot better?

4. Clean and wash your hands. Hmmm, this reminds me of calling my kids to the dinner table. You don't want to bring the dirt of this world to the dinner table and risk getting sick. These are the things that are on the outside that soil our relationship with God.

5. Purify our hearts. Decontaminate, get rid of impurities, cleanse the attitudes, thoughts, desires, mindsets, ways of thinking, feelings, notions, ideas, contemplations, all the ways of who we are on the inside.

6, 7, and 8. Be sad and sorry and weep. This is a triple-header. We need to repent. To turn away from those items that hinder us from our relationship with God. Stop! Turn around! Head back to the cross, get close to God, and draw near to Him.

9 and 10. Direct us to be sober, clear-headed, serious, thoughtful, restrained, and solemn in the seriousness of our sin.

I need to trust Him in times that don't make sense and in those times that it would be easier to lean into my own way of doing things. My old self thought "acorns" tasted good, but in God's kingdom, I know now that they are terrible for me. When I follow God's plan, He will honor and lift me up! I don't know about you, but again, based upon my actions, God says that if I pursue after Him, He will lift me up into eternal existence with Him. I get to live forever with Him!

Prayer

Oh Lord,

Today was a lot to take in. I do want to get up close and personal with You. I desire to live the life that You designed for me and to trust You even when the ways of this world are so different from Yours. Help me to turn away from the things that hinder me. Forgive me. I need to come closer to You to get clean and right. Thank You for loving me. I want to know that I truly know You. Help me to see You clearly and to immerse myself completely in You and Your ways. I want my heart to be totally Yours. I want You with the capital "G," not that little "g" god of my own design. Thank You so very much. I love You. Amen.

> I pray that your love will overflow more and more,
> and that you will keep on growing in knowledge and
> understanding.
> Philippians 1:9 (NLT)

1. Talk with God, get to know him by experience. Get up close and personal.

2. Be devoted to what you know He is.

3. Walk closely with Him.

WEEK THREE

Simply Worship
Day Four

Over the years, I have gone from a dislike to a dependency
upon computers. The dependency is rooted in the fact that I am
a horrible speller. So bad that even spell check has no idea what
I mean at times. Even as a young girl, it used to frustrate me that
a teacher would ask me to look up a word that I did not know
how to spell in the dictionary. If I knew how to spell it, I would
be able to look it up! What were they thinking? With spell check,
I sometimes look up the synonyms in order to figure out how
to spell a word. The bottom line is that if I want to know what
a word means, I have to know how to spell it. If I truly want to
understand its full meaning, I must search out how to spell it, so
I can look up its definition. I know now what the teachers were
thinking; they wanted me to go down the path of learning, not
take the easy road of shortcuts. Shortcuts in life only produce
a shorter understanding and decrease the benefit for our
comprehension.

Worship is a word I can spell, but it means different things
to different people, cultures, and religions. We see this struggle
in the mind of the woman at the well. Let's review John 4:
19-24. First, read this in your own translation. Why your own
translation? Because it is your comfort zone of understanding.
Then, I want to expand our comprehension by looking at the
scripture from another view. Again, remember we want to
understand God in His entirety.

"Oh, so you're a prophet! Well, tell me this: Our ancestors worshiped God at this mountain, but you Jews insist that Jerusalem is the only place for worship, right?"

John 4:19-20 (MSG)

My thought here is that she wants to move on from this conversation because it is making her uncomfortable. Yet, she wants to hear more at the hope that He may know more about God than she does. Remember Jesus just pointed out her current living situation, so she is trying to remove the focus from her to who Jesus is as a Jew and where and how the Jews worshiped. The Samaritans worshiped on Mt. Gerizim, and the Jews worshiped on Mt. Ebal. I find it humorous that some things never change. If you want to harm a relationship with another believer, challenge them that their place and mechanics of worship are in error.

Verses 21-23, "Believe me, woman, the time is coming when you Samaritans will worship the Father neither here at this mountain nor there in Jerusalem." Jesus thus clarifies what is not important when it comes to worship. It is not the "where" of worship but the "whom" of worship. We need to know the object of our worship. Verses 21-23 continued, "You worship guessing in the dark; we Jews worship in the clear light of day. God's way of salvation is made available through the Jews. But the time is coming—it has, in fact, come—when what you're called will not matter and where you go to worship will not matter."

The Samaritans only knew part of God. They actually worshiped the one and only true God but in part. It was like they were standing in a dark room with earplugs crammed snuggly into their ear canals, so close to seeing and hearing God, yet shutting him out. All they or any of us need to do is light a candle and unplug our ears to hear and see what the Lord has to reveal.

Verses 23-24, "It's who you are and the way you live that count before God. Your worship must engage your spirit in the pursuit of truth. That's the kind of people the Father is out looking for: those who are simply and honestly themselves before him in their worship."

Rewrite verses 23-24 in your own words to describe how to worship.

Verses 23-24 continued, "God is sheer being itself—Spirit. Those who worship him must do it out of their very being, their spirits, their true selves, in adoration." I also like the way the NIV says it. Verses 23-24, "Yet a time is coming and has now come when the true worshipers will worship the Father in the Spirit and in truth, for they are the kind of worshipers the Father seeks. God is spirit, and his worshipers must worship in the Spirit and in truth."

To worship in spirit and in truth! It really is not that big of a task. So we know the how and the why. What about the way that leads to worship? Is your spirit engaging in the pursuit of truth?

"Don't let your hearts be troubled. Trust in God, and trust also in me. There is more than enough room in my Father's home. If this were not so, would I have told you that I am going to prepare a place for you? When everything is ready, I will come and get you, so that you will always be with me where I am. And you know the way to where I am going." "No, we don't know, Lord," Thomas said. "We have no idea where you are going, so how can we know the way?"

John 14:1-5 (NLT)

I love this! Old Thomas, also referred to as Didymus, whose name translates in Hebrew and Greek as "twin," has a reputation as a doubter, but because of his twin nature, sometimes also shows courage and devotion. He takes the initiative to ask the way! He isn't thinking about whether he appears stupid by not knowing; he does not know, so he asks. So simple, but too often, we forget to stop and ask for directions.

"Blessed are those who hunger and thirst for righteousness, for they will be filled."

Matthew 5:6 (NKJV)

I don't know about you, but fill me up, Lord! Many years ago, I had the privilege of recommending the name of our church, Crossroads, based upon Jeremiah 6:16.

This is what the Lord says:
Stop at the crossroads and look around.
Ask for the old, godly way, and walk in it.
Travel its path, and you will find rest for your souls.

Jeremiah 6:16 (NIV)

The directions are simple: Stop, look, ask, walk, and then you will find rest. There you have it; you are now "in the know."

> Jesus told him, "I am the way, the truth, and the life. No one can come to the Father except through me. If you had really known me, you would know who my Father is. From now on, you do know him and have seen him!"
>
> John 14:6-7 (NLT)

Now, we are going to the book of 1 John. This is an interesting book because it addresses believers but not anyone at any specific location. So it has a broader audience. I want you to look at chapter 2, verses 1-6; then, fill in the blanks below.

1. John writes the letter to keep us from _____.
2. Our advocate is _____, and He also speaks to the Father for the whole _____.
3. The evidence that we know Him is found in our _____.
4. If we do not keep and do His commands we are _____.
5. I show my love for God by _____.
6. If I live in God, I will _____.

Do you *know* that you know God? If you are not sure, look to the Word of God for the answers, remain in fellowship with other believers, talk to God, and walk as Jesus did. Take a moment before we close today to examine how and who you worship.

Are there things you need to do to return to a place of true and honest worship? Make a list of any changes:

Prayer:

Dear God,

Remind me to stop and ask for directions so that I can walk as Jesus walked and fully receive Your love that You intended for me to receive. I want to simply and honestly worship You. In His love, amen.

WEEK THREE

Situational Awareness

Day Five

The first time that you get up on a horse, with the anticipation of learning how to ride, it can be a little unnerving. Horses are big animals with a lot of strength. It is always wise to have an instructor that can teach you how to ride properly. This investment will save you from frustration and injury.

Avery started the girls out on horses that she knew were tolerant and forgiving of a novice. She also stayed connected to the rider by either walking alongside them or using a lunge line. A lunge line is a twenty-to-thirty-foot line that is connected to the horse's bridle. The instructor will stand in the middle of the arena holding the lunge line in their hand. Horse and rider will then move in a circle around the instructor while connected to this lunge line. The instructor will have the rider practice several drills while sitting in the saddle to develop skills such as strength and balance. Eventually, the riders will let go of the reins, thus forcing themselves to trust the rhythm of the horse rather than their grip on the reins. Knowing where they are in relation to the horse is a very crucial concept to achieve. Avery would watch the girls and make corrections as necessary for the improvement of their balance. As the girls continued to learn, they ultimately rode on their own, with only the wisdom of Avery echoing within their actions. These well-learned lessons became the tools that kept the girls safe when challenging situations occurred.

There is a sort of situational awareness that every rider must develop. Situational awareness is an aviation term used to describe the fact that you need to be aware of what is happening around you at all times. If you are aware of your surroundings, the horse, and your motion, you will be capable of making sound decisions in case of a sudden change in your circumstances. For example, the horse becomes startled by something and suddenly stops. If you are not balanced in your saddle, your forward motion will launch you forward over the horse's head and onto the hard ground with an uncomfortable and sometimes painful thud! The lessons learned on that lunge line provide you with the skill needed for proper balance in all circumstances.

We, too, need to be aware of our situations. As Christians, God has given us an instructor, mentor, teacher, and trainer. The Bible talks about not leaving us unattended or uncared for as believers. Because of the gift of the Holy Spirit, we can maintain situational awareness. Jesus promises to give us an advocate, the Holy Spirit.

> "All this I have spoken while still with you. But the Advocate, the Holy Spirit, whom the Father will send in my name, will teach you all things and will remind you of everything I have said to you. Peace I leave with you; my peace I give you. I do not give to you as the world gives. Do not let your hearts be troubled and do not be afraid."
>
> John 14:25-27 (NIV)

Jesus says to His disciples:

Verse 26: He has provided us with _____.

Verse 27: He gives us _____.

Verse 27: We need not be _____ or _____

Now, read verses 28-31 in your own Bible.

Verse 28: Jesus is _____ back.

Verse 30: The enemy has no _____ over Him.

Scrutinize closely the "situational awareness" revealed to us by Jesus in regards to the Holy Spirit.

> But very truly I tell you, it is for your good that I
> am going away. Unless I go away, the Advocate will
> not come to you; but if I go, I will send him to you.
> When he comes, he will prove the world to be in the
> wrong about sin and righteousness and judgment:
> about sin, because people do not believe in me; about
> righteousness, because I am going to the Father, where
> you can see me no longer; and about judgment, because
> the prince of this world now stands condemned.
> "I have much more to say to you, more than you can
> now bear. But when he, the Spirit of truth, comes, he
> will guide you into all the truth. He will not speak on
> his own; he will speak only what he hears, and he will
> tell you what is yet to come. He will glorify me because
> it is from me that he will receive what he will make
> known to you. All that belongs to the Father is mine.
> That is why I said the Spirit will receive from me what
> he will make known to you."
>
> John 16:7-15 (NIV)

Jesus says in verses 7-12:

1. It is _____ that He left His disciples.

2. When Jesus is gone, He will send the _____.

3. The Spirit will reveal the truth about:

a. _____ b. _____ c. _____

4. The Spirit will (v. 13):

a. _____ b. _____

c. _____ d. _____

Then, in verse 14, Jesus, referring to the Holy Spirit, says, "He will glorify me because it is from me that he will receive what he will make known to you." Here is the key to unlocking the door to understanding and comprehending what it is we need to believe and stand steadfast in our faith. God, our Father, sent Jesus to pay the price for our sins. Jesus then returns to heaven but takes care of us by sending us the Holy Spirit to guide and instruct us. So back to the original question of this week, "How do you know that you know God?" We know God because He gave us the Spirit to give us peace of mind and heart, to keep us from being troubled or afraid. Because we know that the enemy has no power over Jesus and that He is coming back to bring us to our heavenly home!

> The woman said, "I know the Messiah is coming—the one who is called Christ. When he comes, he will explain everything to us." Then Jesus told her, "I Am the Messiah!"
>
> John 4:25-26 (NLT)

Prayer

Thank You, Father God, for sending Your Holy Spirit to guide and teach me the things that I need to know about being Your child. I love You and want to follow the instructions that You give me through Your written Word and the Holy Spirit. Help me to remain confident in the fact that because of Your spirit, I know that I can know You! In the power of the name of Jesus, amen.

WEEK FOUR

The Light, Life, and Love of the Lord

There is this incredible stark difference between light and dark, life and death. Yet sometimes, we get so caught up in our daily routines that we do not take notice of the contrast. Unless we see the dark foreboding shadows of this world, we forget that life is fragile. Empty people are void of the life-giving love of God. If we don't take time to pause from our busy agendas, we may miss some amazing opportunities. If we become imbalanced, we can be kept from our Father's work. It is good to be about the tasks that please God, not those that keep us busy. I am talking about the mission we have been assigned to bring the empty people from that darkness into the light. To help those who are void of life to bathe themselves in the joy and love of the living waters of God. I want to sear upon our hearts a desire or, better yet, a passion for the empty. We need a passion to help others discover the light, life, and love of the Lord.

WEEK FOUR

The Mission

Day One

The legendary Pony Express. Just the name sends images racing across my mind. These men who rode from coast to coast had purpose. Their mission was to deliver the United States mail. They even had an oath of conduct as follows:

Pony Express: The Oath of Employment

"I _____ do hereby swear, before the great and living God, that during my engagement, and while I am an employee of Russell, Majors & Waddell, I will, under no circumstances, use profane language. I will drink no intoxicating liquors; that I will not quarrel or fight with any other employee of the firm, and that in every respect, I will conduct myself honestly, faithful to my duties, and so direct my acts as to win the confidence of my employers. So help me God."

Ponyexpress.org

We also have a mission; our mission is to love God and others. If we step out to reach others for the Lord, He is faithful to provide a way for us to serve Him; I love that about God. Take a look around you, at your family, group of friends, and those in your sphere of influence. I am confident that they are all there because God placed you where He designed you to serve. Stop and think about that for a moment. If you are where God wants you, then they must be too. If God is God, which I am convinced that He is, then He has purpose in all that He does!

So who are the empty that you are praying for? If you did not make a list of names, do so now. It is okay to re-evaluate that list. Pray and ask God to give you the names that belong on your list. Just think of the opportunities that God has for you to love others!

My list:

Paul authored the book of Ephesians. Before we look at it today, I want to take a little time to ask ourselves, "What was the reason for this letter to the Ephesians by Paul?" Ephesus was a large type of trade and commercial center situated on a busy river port. Thus, people from different areas came to trade their goods. It also boasted of a Pagan temple that was dedicated to the Roman goddess Diana. Paul was a genius! All he had to do for three years was stay put, and the people who were empty came to him. Today Ephesus is located in what is known as Turkey. I want to look at a few details in the opening of this book to build a foundation.

> Paul, an apostle of Christ Jesus by the will of God, To
> God's holy people in Ephesus, the faithful in Christ
> Jesus: Grace and peace to you from God our Father
> and the Lord Jesus Christ. Praise for Spiritual Blessings
> in Christ Praise be to the God and Father of our Lord
> Jesus Christ, who has blessed us in the heavenly realms
> with every spiritual blessing in Christ.
>
> Ephesians 1:1-3 (NIV)

What is an apostle? An apostle, according to the Greek, is a
sort of missionary or delegate sent by someone else for a special
purpose. In Paul's case, this special sender is Christ. Paul had
strong beliefs and convictions and knew that He was called to
share His message. Next, we notice that he is addressing God's
holy people or saints. To be holy is a special description of
believers. The believers are those who have confirmed Christ as
their Savior. As a result, God has given us "every spiritual blessing
in Christ." Now that has got to make you feel warm all over! Now,
with your eyes set on alert for those who are empty, let's read the
Word of God together.

> Once you were dead because of your disobedience and
> your many sins. You used to live in sin, just like the rest
> of the world, obeying the devil—the commander of the
> powers in the unseen world. He is the spirit at work in
> the hearts of those who refuse to obey God. All of us
> used to live that way, following the passionate desires
> and inclinations of our sinful nature. By our very nature
> we were subject to God's anger, just like everyone else.
>
> Ephesians 2:1-3 (NLT)

1._____ is at work in the hearts of those in the world.

2. They are following the _____ desires and _____ of their sinful nature.

3. What does it mean to have passionate desires and inclinations?

4. Can you remember what it felt like to be under such bondage?

Oppressed and burdened with the things that hinder us from living the life that we were designed to live. It was horrible. It was like the horse eating the acorns. She had a hunger for what made her deathly ill. Ask God to give you what I call a "God heart and mind" for those who are burdened. They are the portals to help you see and understand those who are hampered by the limited vision of darkness.

Ephesians 2:4-10 (NLT)

But God is so rich in mercy, and he loved us so much, that even though we were dead because of our sins, he gave us life when he raised Christ from the dead. (It is only by God's grace that you have been saved!) For he raised us from the dead along with Christ and seated us with him in the heavenly realms because we are united with Christ Jesus. So God can point to us in all future ages as examples of the incredible wealth of his grace and kindness toward us, as shown in all he has done for us who are united with Christ Jesus. God saved you by his grace when you believed. And you can't take credit for this; it is a gift from God. Salvation is not a reward for the good things we have done, so none of us can boast about it. For we are God's masterpiece. He has created us anew in Christ Jesus, so we can do the good things he planned for us long ago.

5. We, as God's _____, can do the _____ things He _____ for us long ago (verse 10).

Don't you think that those on your list would like to become God's masterpiece, His stunning success too?

What are some of the parts of verses 4-10 that you think will help you to be a stunning success?

My list of things to help become a stunning success:

Let's review a familiar verse, John 3:16-17 (NLT),

> For God so loved the world that he gave his one and
> only Son, that whoever believes in him shall not perish
> but have eternal life. For God did not send his Son into
> the world to condemn the world, but to save the world
> through him.

I want you to contemplate what you consider to be the
good plans that God has for you, as "His delegate" of the saving
message of Jesus, as found in John 3:16-17. Now write it out in
your own words as a plan for you in the mission field of the time
and place that God has planted you.

My plan:

In the verses that follow, John 3:18-21, they spell out the difference between who we were and who we are at present.

Please read in your Bible, then answer the following questions.

Verse 18: Who is judged?

Verse 19-20: What is the purpose of the light?

Who are the people that hate the light?

Verse 21: Who comes into the light and for what purpose?

Why do people stay in the dark? Stir up some love for those on your list from week one, day three and write down some ways that you can help them to come into the light of God's love. I would like to give you a hint; this is the chapter before the woman at the well!

I want to help those on my list by:

Prayer:

Dear Lord,

Help me to become Your missionary for those on my list, to introduce them to Your love through the saving grace found in Jesus. You have placed me exactly where I need to be for this time in history, alongside those who need to be brought into the light. Help me to be like Paul and reach those who You have placed within my sphere of influence. Sear on my heart a love for the lost on my list. Amen.

Contrasts

Day Two

Bad behavior is manifested in personality and lifestyle. A horse with bad behavior is obviously annoying and sometimes dangerous. Stable vices come in many forms, cribbing, weaving, bolting food, kicking, biting, pawing, and digging the stall floor. These habits or vices develop over time, usually due to boredom. An average stall is about a ten-by-twelve-foot space. If possible, an adjacent paddock with a minimum of six hundred square feet is nice to have. That is not much for an animal that was designed to roam and graze! Could you imagine being in a confined area like that? I recently traveled for twenty-one hours, and I thought I was going to leap out of my skin. If it had lasted any longer, I would have developed some very annoying behaviors!

When a horse exhibits a vice on the trail or in the arena, that is when things can get dangerous for the rider. They include bucking, crow hopping, rolling, loose saddles that come off when mounted due to sucking air, rearing, not paying attention, I could go on and on. These develop as a result of a response to a situation that actually results in a desired outcome for the horse. For example, a timid horse that is afraid of bridges has learned that if it rears before having to cross, it can lose its rider and be able to avoid the undesired experience. If I discipline by a painful stimulus, it can reinforce the experience as awful. So knowing that the animal is fearful of bridges, I can dismount and lead my horse across the bridge. The horse learns that the bridge is nothing to fear. With time, I can replace the bad behavior with good behavior.

Life seems to be full of contrasts: light versus darkness, life versus death, hot versus cold, or old versus young. The Bible also has extremes listed, as we have been discussing Spirit-led life in contrast to our sinful desires. The Bible speaks about these as good and bad fruit. Remember the verses from yesterday in Ephesians?

> Praise be to the God and Father of our Lord Jesus Christ, who has blessed us in the heavenly realms with every spiritual blessing in Christ.
>
> Ephesians 1:3 (NIV)

> For we are God's masterpiece. He has created us anew in Christ Jesus, so we can do the good things he planned for us long ago.
>
> Ephesians 2:10 (NLT)

As God's masterpiece, we are blessed with every spiritual blessing for the purpose of what good works He has planned for us to do. We are to be His stunning success! He will not take you to that fearful bridge and beat you into submission. God is love, and He desires to love us through the fearful times. As we learn to replace our learned bad habits with good conduct, we become closer to being what He created us to be. He wants to soothe us with the encouragement of His Word.

Open your Bible and read Galatians 5:16-24.

I like to start out on the right foot, so first, list the fruit of the spirit from verses 22 and 23.

List the fruits of the spirit:

1._____ 2._____ 3._____ 4._____

5._____ 6._____ 7._____ 8._____

9._____

We are told in the previous verses 16-18 (NCV):

> So I tell you: Live by following the Spirit. Then you will not do what your sinful selves want. Our sinful selves want what is against the Spirit, and the Spirit wants what is against our sinful selves. The two are against each other, so you cannot do just what you please. But if the Spirit is leading you, you are not under the law.

Rewrite in your own words verses 16-18:

God's Word warns us about the behaviors that we should not exhibit in verses 19-21 (NCV):

> The wrong things the sinful self does are clear: being sexually unfaithful, not being pure, taking part in sexual sins, worshiping gods, doing witchcraft, hating, making trouble, being jealous, being angry, being selfish, making people angry with each other, causing divisions among people, feeling envy, being drunk, having wild and wasteful parties, and doing other things like these. I warn you now as I warned you before: Those who do these things will not inherit God's kingdom.

Now, make a list of the fruit of our sinful nature:

1._____ 2._____ 3._____ 4._____

5._____ 6._____ 7._____ 8._____

9._____ 10._____ 11. _____

12._____13._____ 14._____

I want to back up again:

> For you have been called to live in freedom, my brothers and sisters. But don't use your freedom to satisfy your sinful nature. Instead, use your freedom to serve one another in love. For the whole law can be summed up in this one command: "Love your neighbor as yourself." But if you are always biting and devouring one another, watch out! Beware of destroying one another.
>
> Galatians 5:13-25 (NLT)

1. We are called to _____.

2. To use this freedom to_____.

3. The law is summed up to _____.

The above verses are expressed again in Colossians:

> God has chosen you and made you his holy people. He loves you. So you should always clothe yourselves with mercy, kindness, humility, gentleness, and patience. Bear with each other, and forgive each other. If someone does wrong to you, forgive that person because the Lord forgave you. Even more than all this, clothe yourself in love. Love is what holds you all together in perfect unity. Let the peace that Christ gives control your thinking, because you were all called together in one body to have peace. Always be thankful. Let the teaching of Christ live in you richly. Use all wisdom to teach and instruct each other by singing psalms, hymns, and spiritual songs with thankfulness in your hearts to God. Everything you do or say should be done to obey Jesus your Lord. And in all you do, give thanks to God the Father through Jesus.
>
> Colossians 3:12-17 (NCV)

Wow! What if we all lived this way? Stop, pray, then reread the above verses. Now, think for a moment of what God, through His instruction manual, is trying to tell you.

Make a list of six points that you would like to adopt as "good behavior" in your life.

1.

2.

3.

4.

5.

6.

> For you were once darkness, but now you are light in the Lord. Live as children of light (for the fruit of the light consists in all goodness, righteousness and truth) and find out what pleases the Lord.
>
> Ephesians 5:8-10 (NIV)

The tree and its fruit are described in Matthew 7:15-23. Please read in your own Bible. Then rewrite this in your own words:

Our Lord talked about filling our water jars with the "living water" in John chapter 4. The woman at the well for many years had filled her water jar with the things of this world. Her fruit, as a result, was rotten and thorny. She thought she had the right water due to the teaching she received as a Samaritan. Would she hear the words, "I never knew you. Get away from me, you who break God's laws"? If she doesn't look deep into the well of "living water," she will. She, like us, needs to fill that jar with the good, loving fruit that the spirit offers to those who thirst after it.

Prayer:

Oh Father God, help me to thirst after You and to fill my jar of life only with the fruit of Your Spirit. You have so much to offer me from Your living well. Help me not to shy away but to lean into it with all my strength! Amen.

Shine Your Light

Day Three

Leading by example is a fantastic way to teach a principle. To "pony" a horse or horses, you bring them alongside or behind the horse that you are riding. The ponied horse in need of training is attached to a halter with a long lead rope. It is important when training to be mounted on a well-trained, calm, and gentle horse. This good, solid, forgiving horse, which tolerates the trainee's lack of manners, is the best type of mount to have. Another good way to train a foal is to have the foal follow its mother. An example of this is that a good mare could teach her foal how to load in a trailer faster than we could. The mare is impressing upon its foal that it is okay to load into a scary tin can. If the mare is calm and shows no fear, the foal will accept this as something to be explored and done.

We, too, are to be examples, bringing others along the side of us, helping them to discover the ways of the Lord, allowing them to follow, and impressing upon their hearts the love of the Lord by our actions. We want them to see the fingerprints of God in and all over our lives. I have heard it said and know it to be true that sometimes the only Jesus others may see is the Jesus that we reflect in our lives by our actions. We, by doing what the Word of God tells us to do, reflect the love of God into the lives of others. We need to maintain the training we received when we were brought alongside other believers. The woman at the well had the opportunity to learn from the Master; we have been given the Holy Spirit as our trainer. You and I are in training to become the people of God we were created to be, so here are some good principles to hold unto. We are going to talk about how we can be better examples by adding salt and light to the lives of others. Take out your Bible and read Matthew 5:13-16, then we will review the verses together.

> "You are the salt of the earth; but if the salt has become tasteless, how can it be made salty again? It is no longer good for anything, except to be thrown out and trampled under foot by men."
>
> Matthew 5:13 (NASB)

Salt has many qualities that are and were very valuable. Salt is a mineral known as sodium chloride and was sought after for preserving food, adding flavor, and medicinal purposes. Our bodies also require salt as part of their electrolyte balance. Salt, that simple ingredient, is a vital part of life!

The two points that I would like to talk about are preservation and flavor. To preserve is to protect, conserve, and safeguard. These are qualities we need to be careful that we show evidence of in our lives as Christians. We all have those attributes of who we are that need to be brought into focus, re-evaluated, and examined for effectiveness in service of others, just like the horse that is of use to train other horses because of its attributes of quality.

What do you need to preserve in your walk so that you can serve others?

The second point is flavor. I love food with flavor, lots of flavor! Flavor, taste, tang, spice, zest, all of these add so much to the food we eat. Well-seasoned food is simply amazing! When I am busy cooking dinner, the aroma of flavors and spices draws my family into the kitchen to take a taste of what is being prepared. We want to draw others to Jesus.

When you first came to understand the amazing qualities of the "living water," what was it that you saw in the lifestyle of the believer that drew you to Jesus? What was the "zest for life" that they knew and you wanted a taste of?

List three things that drew you to the Lord:

1.

2.

3.

Matthew was a tax collector, hated among the people of his time. Have you ever been disliked or hated by others? It is a very lonely and horrible feeling. A feeling of being left out and loathed can conjure up very dark emotions in one's heart. Yet, as hated as he was, the flavor and light that Jesus gave to others enticed this man to God.

Light also has many characteristics necessary for life. The most obvious is the illumination qualities. Have you ever been on a tour of a cave? I took a cave tour once, and the guide took us all to a rather large underground cavern. He then had the lights that were illuminating this cavern turned off suddenly. What an incredible moment! First, you heard a "gasp," then silence, and finally, a little shuffling of feet. When the lights came back on, there were two responses observed. Either people had huddled together for security, or they were standing with their arms out, looking for something solid.

We need light. We need to see the clarity of it in our lives, just like we need to feel the solid and stable attributes of God. Remember that God has given us His Spirit, the Holy Spirit, to guide us.

> "You are the light of the world—like a city on a hilltop that cannot be hidden. No one lights a lamp and then puts it under a basket. Instead, a lamp is placed on a stand, where it gives light to everyone in the house. In the same way, let your good deeds shine out for all to see, so that everyone will praise your heavenly Father."
>
> Matthew 5:14-16 (NLT)

Jesus tells us in John 8:12 (NLT), "I am the light of the world. If you follow me, you won't have to walk in darkness, because you will have the light that leads to life."

Read Mark 4:21-25 in your Bible, then answer the following questions.

1. Where do people place lamps and why?

2. What are some of the ways you can shine for others?

3. What will happen to the things that we hide?

Rewrite verses 24-25 in your own words:

I had an accident one time while camping. I was walking at night, and I was holding my flashlight as I walked, looking ahead of me about fifteen feet. Smack! Down I went into a large, unused, metal fire ring. I managed to come down on my shin, and I bear the dent in my bone to this day. The problem was this; I was not looking where I was going. *Wait a minute; you just said that you had a flashlight.* Well, I did, but I was looking too far ahead. I needed to look at where my feet were going. In Psalm 119:105 (NIV), David states, "Your word is a lamp for my feet, a light on my path." David knew that to cast light on his feet was all that he needed. In other words, you trust God for the steps that you are taking, and He will handle what is down the path. He has given us His Spirit as the lamp or flashlight for our travels down the path of life.

Can you describe a time when you were looking too far down the path?

Proverbs 20:27 (NIV) states:

> The human spirit is the lamp of the LORD that sheds light on one's inmost being.

Think about that for a moment. The proverbs are wise words to help strengthen who we are as the children of God. We just learned that the light is going to expose the darkness. Remember that Jesus told the woman at the well in verses 22-24 that they worshiped what they did not know. Shinning light on the subject, He cleared that misunderstanding. He wants to illuminate our paths just like He was shedding light on the path of the woman at the well. He was helping her to discover God as her Father.

So how do you *know* that you know God?

Finally, look up Psalm 18:28-36 and read and contemplate the song that David was singing and praising to God. Did you know that psalms were songs of praise to God?

There are two things going on in this praise. One is "who God is," and the other is "what God does" for David and us. Now, I want you to write your own praise to God for who He is and what He has done for you! Then, close in your own prayer to Him.

My praise

My prayer

THIRSTY

Working Together in Love
Day Four

The end of summer always brings the county fair. My children were often involved, and it was a very busy weekend. There are the 4-H exhibits, wonderfully bad food that tastes so good at the time, the "who is who" of the area, a parade, sheepdog trials, and of course, a good old fashion rodeo. The rodeo, what a time of fun! The rodeo always would start out with the parade of champions. This is where all the white and green uniforms from 4-H show their winning animals. Children and youth of all ages display their animals to the spectators in the grandstands. Then, the rodeo would commence with the usual events. Then, at halftime, the presentation of the American flag by the drill team on horseback is my favorite. This is the type of moment that your heart beats faster, and you feel your buttons pop for a feeling of "I am glad to be an American." It really is a spectacular event. What makes this so amazing is the unity of the horses and riders.

If you have time, look up a clip of an equestrian drill team on the Internet. The ladies are all decked out in identical riding uniforms and ride in synchronized maneuvers to music. Thundering into the arena at full gallop with flags waving, they split into two groups that weave in and out of each other. If their timing is off, a mid-event collision could be disastrous. Trust me when I tell you that these animals and riders are very well trained. They practice for hours as a group and individually with their horse. When they come together at the fair, it is a dazzling moment to view. They become so cohesive and harmonized that the flow of their movement is as if they are one unit.

We, too, as believers, are to work together as one unit. We are to all have a heart for the Lord because an independent mindset in the arena of a Christian life can cause chaos.

I have seen individuals in a church with their own agendas cause disaster within a body of believers. If we look up to the Master, taking His wisdom inward to our hearts and minds, then we produce an outward component of precision. A believer is so focused on God that they work and live together as one body, the body of Christ Jesus, our Lord.

Time to look to the Bible for some wisdom. Read 1 Corinthians 12:12-26. Take note that this is preceding the chapter all about what love is and what love is not. So read and then look up to the Lord for a light to shine inward on your mind and heart regarding the words we will read today. Then, let them overflow outward unto others by example.

1. We are part of _____ body and baptized by _____ spirit. (Verses 12-13)

2. Even though we may be _____ parts, we are still part of _____ body. (Verses 12-13)

3. God has placed each part of the _____ exactly where He _____ it to be. (Verses 15-19)

4. Again, God says that there are _____ parts but only one _____. (Verse 20)

5. He is making a point here; take note of it and listen! We can never tell another part of the body that we _____ need them. (Verses 21-22)

6. We, as members of the body, need to _____ each other. (Verses 24-25)

7. If one suffers, all _____ . If one part is _____, all are honored. (Verse 26)

This is again astounding wisdom for us to take into our hearts and minds. I also think that Galatians 5:13-14 (NIV) answers the question on how to live by the Spirit, "You, my brothers and sisters, were called to be free. But do not use your freedom to indulge the flesh; rather, serve one another humbly in love. For the entire law is fulfilled in keeping this one command: 'Love your neighbor as yourself.'"

So who is your neighbor? Is it one of the people on your list? Someone who is close to you in location usually defines a neighbor. In today's world of instant communication, a close friend or neighbor can be anywhere. Think about those on your list and their need to be loved. Everyone has a need to belong and be loved.

Can you describe how the Lord would have you "love your neighbor as yourself"?

How might a love that is to be an example of God's love look like to someone who is on your list? Describe how you can apply this to your list of people:

Back to the book of John, this time chapter 15:12-17.

> "This is My commandment, that you love one another, just as I have loved you. Greater love has no one than this, that one lay down his life for his friends."
>
> John 15: 12-13 (NASB)

Here is an example of God's love for us in the fact that He gave us His Son for us. Crucifixion was a horrible death. They would lay down the wooden cross on the ground and nail someone to it. So this verse is referring to the fact that Jesus was laid down and was crucified for your sins. He laid down His life for you on that cross. So we, too, are to die to ourselves for others. This means to lay down the items that keep you from loving and serving. Then, you will be free from the attitudes, feelings, thoughts, and actions that keep you from putting someone else first. A part of the body cannot be independent; it needs to work together with the other parts. Your neighbor needs you to put aside yourself and love them the way God would have you love them.

What are the things in your life that maintain you as a slave to selfishness?

"You are My friends if you do what I command you."

John 15:14 (NASB)

This is an interesting requirement. The word "command" in the old French means "enjoin, to attach." If I follow God's instructions, I "attach" to my leader. An officer may have an "attachment" to soldiers. In other words, by following the instructions given to me, I become "joined" to the one who has the information needed to succeed, which is leading me in the direction that I need to follow.

> "No longer do I call you slaves, for the slave does not know what his master is doing; but I have called you friends, for all things that I have heard from My Father I have made known to you."
>
> John 15:15 (NASB)

Some translations use the word "servant" instead of "slave"; the meaning or inference is to be understood as someone who follows the orders given without having to understand the rationale. Back to the drill team, each team has a leader. The leader is responsible for ensuring that the team members understand the instructions regarding the different maneuvers to be performed. This is very crucial. If they misunderstand a command, it could result in a harmful collision. The team leader may use a whistle in the arena so that the riders can hear the cues and follow through with their instruction so that the team completes their routine. The rider will then give a cue to the horse, and the animal will then follow through with a learned behavior. The horse has learned to perform a behavior as a result of a learned response.

> "You did not choose Me but I chose you, and appointed you that you would go and bear fruit, and that your fruit would remain, so that whatever you ask of the Father in My name He may give to you. This I command you, that you love one another."
>
> John 15:16-17 (NASB)

Jesus is speaking to His disciples in the upper room right after He had washed their feet. If you want to read more about this, start with chapter 13 of the book of John. It will give you a better understanding. The student would typically choose the rabbi that they desired to teach them the Torah and Law. Jesus is turning the tables here and has chosen the students. This is the exciting part of that choice. He has a purpose for this choice that they will produce much fruit! The fruit that takes root in love would go forth to serve others for God. So remember that when we engage the Lord like the woman at the well, we are searching and questioning what we know. Then, we can exchange what we know for the truth of God. The Lord will illuminate us with His truth so we can carry out His commands!

Prayer

Dear Lord,

I want to serve You. I want to work together as one unit with the body of believers to serve others as You would serve with love. That the fruit yielded would be evident of the spirit that lives in me. Oh Lord, how I love You and thank You for Your patience with me as I grow up in You and You alone. I want You to be my teacher, and I shall be Your student. Teach me, Lord, to be more and more like You. Amen.

Remember: If we look up to the Master, taking His wisdom inward to our hearts and minds, then we produce an outward component of precision. A believer that is so focused on God that they work and live together as one body, the body of Christ Jesus our Lord. Amen.

WEEK FOUR

Knock, Knock
Day Five

When I look at the woman at the well, I see a woman who still has a measure of hope left. A hope that life could be different. Some would look at her as a woman who is calloused and hardened from years of sin. She does not shut down the conversation with Jesus, although she may challenge Him. Does she dare to hope that things could be different? She may, at first, desire the living water so she won't have to come back to the well for her daily supply. But this shows a desire for answers to an improved life. She has the hope that even she could achieve a satisfied life. She is persistent and has a tenacity to hang on. Jesus is that hope that things could be different than the broken life that she lives. Jesus is engaging her to look deeply into "the well of her life" and the comparison to what could be if she drank instead from the well of "living water" that He had to offer. Hope, what an amazing promise of God. This woman...dares to hope. She challenges. She has tenacity. She is persistent.

1. What does it mean to have hope?

2. What do you look forward to in your future?

3. Define "persistent":

Jesus answered her, "If you knew the gift of God and who it is that asks you for a drink, you would have asked him and he would have given you living water." "Sir," the woman said, "you have nothing to draw with and the well is deep. Where can you get this living water? Are you greater than our father Jacob, who gave us the well and drank from it himself, as did also his sons and his livestock?" Jesus answered, "Everyone who drinks this water will be thirsty again, but whoever drinks the water I give them will never thirst. Indeed, the water I give them will become in them a spring of water welling up to eternal life." The woman said to him, "Sir, give me this water so that I won't get thirsty and have to keep coming here to draw water."

John 4:10-15 (NIV)

We are over halfway through this study, and we need to keep going to complete the series. Tenacity to complete a project or goal is an attitude that we should all strive to achieve. Jesus loved to encourage His disciples (those who sought His teaching, His followers) by telling them parables. A parable is a story or object lesson used to illustrate a message of moral significance. These parables were used to encourage His followers to be steadfast in the hope of God's plan for their lives. No matter how rough it got, God was there for them and would provide their every need. I want us to take a look at another example of a woman who would not give up.

Read Luke 18:1-8 in your Bible.

1. Jesus used this parable to teach His disciples to _____ and _____. (Verse 1)

2. We see two different types of people characterized in verses 2-3. They were a judge who _____ about people and did not _____ God and a widow.

The widow was seeking _____.

3. In verses 4-5, why did the judge decide to give the widow what she was looking for?

4. Describe in your own words what the Lord wanted us to learn from verses 6-8:

Can you imagine the conversations this widow had with herself every day as she walked to see the judge? I imagine that it went something like this, "Okay, today when the judge looks down his nose at me, I will not be discouraged. I will hold steadfast to my need for justice!" It would be very daunting to face that unyielding judge on a daily basis. There are a couple of points here I want to focus our attention on. Let's look at Luke 18:6-8 (NCV):

> The Lord said, "Listen to what the unfair judge said. God will always give what is right to his people who cry to him night and day, and he will not be slow to answer them. I tell you, God will help his people quickly. But when the Son of Man comes again, will he find those on earth who believe in him?"

List the three main points:

1.

2.

3.

Now, take a closer look at the question asked at the end of verse 8. This is an interesting question to be asking His disciples. This parable has a very important reason for the survival of Christianity over the centuries. The chapter opens up in verse 1 (NIV) with this statement, "Then Jesus told his disciples a parable to show them that they should always pray and not give up." So if we take out the middle of this "sandwich of verses," we have this important message found in the bread of life.

This is what I hear the Lord saying, written in my own words:

> Pray always and don't give up in your requests. Keep asking because when I return, I want to know that the believers of your time will have been encouraged by you. And those who follow will not give up! Times will and can get tough, and you will need to be in communication with Me. I want to always be in contact with you, so talk with Me while I am in heaven, pray, ask Me to answer your prayers; I care that this world is not always right because of the evil judges. But your hope is that I am with you. I am just a prayer away!

I tell you that I have learned to trust and hope in the Lord over the years. And my biggest joy is the prayer life that I have with the Lord! I talk to God all the time. Not only am I connecting, but also because of this connection, I am filled with His love. I am drawing from the living water, and I am not thirsty for what the world has to offer.

Read Luke 11:1-4. The disciples have asked the Lord how they should pray. After reading, rewrite this section in your own words:

Did you mention our daily dependence on the Lord? Note the importance of talking to God about our sins. What do you think He meant? Have we not already been forgiven when we accepted Jesus as the Son of God? The answer is yes! Yet, we live in a world that is not right with God; it is full of those who eat the "acorns of life." We are not perfect; we still need our Savior to take care of us on a daily basis. Our God is holy; His name is hallowed, and in connecting with God, we need to tell Him that we are sorry for the times we eat the acorns of this world or we put ourselves first before Him. Then, we are to forgive others that have wronged us, just like Jesus forgave us. When we do this, it is making ourselves right with God.

> Then Jesus said to them, "Suppose one of you went to your friend's house at midnight and said to him, 'Friend, loan me three loaves of bread. A friend of mine has come into town to visit me, but I have nothing for him

WEEK FOUR • DAY FIVE

to eat.' Your friend inside the house answers, 'Don't bother me! The door is already locked, and my children and I are in bed. I cannot get up and give you anything.' I tell you, if friendship is not enough to make him get up to give you the bread, your boldness will make him get up and give you whatever you need."

Luke 11:5-8 (NCV)

Describe what you think the lesson Jesus is teaching:

"So I tell you to ask and you will receive, search and you will find, knock and the door will be opened for you. Everyone who asks will receive, everyone who searches will find, and the door will be opened for everyone who knocks. Which one of you fathers would give your hungry child a snake if the child asked for a fish? Which one of you would give your child a scorpion if the child asked for an egg? As bad as you are, you still know how to give good gifts to your children. But your heavenly Father is even more ready to give the Holy Spirit to anyone who asks."

Luke 11:9-13 (CEV)

1. What question do you need to start asking?

2. If you were to start searching tomorrow, what would you hope to find?

3. You're knocking at the door, and as Jesus promises, it opens. What is on the other side of that door for you?

Remember the thirsty horse in the pasture, "knock, knock, knock"; she didn't give up until we filled the water trough. God wants to fill your trough; be persistent and do not give up. Ask, seek, and knock! God wants to hear from you! Write your own prayer today based upon something you need to trust and hope in the Lord today.

Prayer:

Dear Lord,

I want to learn how to pray without giving up. I want to have a treasured prayer life with You. Help me to pray. I come to You now with a heart that is searching for answers to the following (you insert here your dialogue with your loving Father):

Additional verses to study:

Psalm 25:20-22

Psalm 31:23-24

Ephesians 1:18-23

Ephesians 5:1-1

Ephesians 6:12

WEEK FIVE

Head to Toe, Inside, and Out

If I were to ask what a healthy horse looked like, you may or may not be able to come up with some details. As an owner of horses, I have learned to apply my nursing skills to doing a head-to-toe, inside-and-out assessment of the health of the horse. It is an evaluation starting at the top and working your way down, looking for any indication that something is not right. We call these signs and symptoms of disease.

Vet checks are an annual event for horses. They receive needed vaccinations and a head-to-toe evaluation. It is at this time that the veterinarian may catch or help prevent something from going wrong. For example, horses, as they age, need to have their teeth floated. It is a filing down of an irregular growth pattern of their teeth that disrupts their ability to properly chew their feed. Improperly ground feed may result in malnutrition. Two of the signs and symptoms are dull coat and weight loss. The problem is that those two symptoms can be evidence of other disorders. For example, a bad case of worms, low-quality feed, or even old age can exhibit the same two symptoms. This is why bringing in the professional to do the very important head-to-toe, inside-and-out assessment is so valuable.

Keeping healthy, whether horse, rider, or believer, is not always an easy task. We tend to keep our outer appearance maintained better than the inner. If what is on the outside is "looking good," we can, unfortunately, let what is on the inside go. We may think that we are doing well, but like anything, bad health habits can sneak up on us. And here is the key; once you understand the disorder that has developed, you need to want to get well. In my nursing career and on our ranch, half of the health issues of a living being are the desire for a state of well-being. A desire to be as healthy as possible is necessary to get well. In other words, we need to identify the problem, desire to see it resolved, and accept the treatment. So what does a healthy Christian look like? Would you be able to recognize the sign and symptoms of a healthy versus unhealthy walk with the Lord? What are the signs and symptoms of a heart for Jesus?

The Treasure Hunt

Day One

To be in balance, you need some sense of stability. God created this world with a need to maintain equilibrium. For example, as a horse breathes in, it takes in oxygen, and then, as it exhales, the horse's body rids itself of the carbon dioxide that it doesn't need. There are all sorts of other internal balances that need to be maintained. Fluid balance is also very important to our survival. All life, from the smallest cell to a horse, needs to stabilize the delicate fluid equilibrium of its existence. If a horse does not get enough water, as I mentioned before, dehydration can develop into colic. We talked about colic and its consequences due to eating too much of the wrong things and the intestinal blockage that can follow. When a horse does not drink enough water, dehydration and its metabolic havoc begin a dreadful scenario. Colic pain in the abdomen is the result of being constipated from lack of hydration. When the pain in its gut starts, a horse will lie down and roll to try and ease the discomfort. Because their gut is heavy and poorly attached, this rolling can cause a twist in the bowel. Circulation is cut off to that section of the gut, and it quickly dies. Gangrene sets in very rapidly, and death is inevitable. It is a very agonizing thing to watch a horse in such pain.

As the caregiver of the horse, I need to watch my animal for signs of dehydration. I can see if the skin "tents up" when I pinch it or whether it goes back to normal. The manure becomes hard and dry and will bounce when it hits the ground. At this point, intervention needs to take place. You need to restore the fluid balance of that horse.

We, as Christians, need to keep our balance. If we indulge ourselves with the "acorns of life," we can become dehydrated in our walks as believers. If we don't keep well supplied with the right things, we will dry up and be of no use. We will become weak and empty. The Bible speaks to the believers about keeping balanced. Here are three points that I would like to talk about. First, we need to connect to God; second, we need to carefully select what we deem as important; and last, we need to keep balanced health by monitoring what we allow to come in. What is in your "water jar"? The woman at the well filled her jar with what she thought to be the right substance to keep her going until Jesus came and showed her the well of living water. John 15:1-11. Jesus is the true vine that keeps the vital fluids necessary for the plant to survive.

Read this section of verses in your Bible, then answer the questions below.

1. Who is the gardener?

2. What is the gardener's job?

3. Who is the vine?

4. What is the purpose of remaining attached to the vine?

5. Who are the branches?

6. What if the branch becomes detached?

7. What are the benefits to the branches if they remain attached to the vine?

8. Who are the true disciples?

So how does a branch get separated from the vine? In verse
one, it says that God cuts out those who do not produce fruit.
So here, a circle of events occurs; our actions and decisions are
what determine our fruitfulness. It is who we are as believers that
determines our attachment to the vine. Remaining attached is
being connected to the source. The woman at the well becomes
attached to the source when she drinks the living water. Without
being united to the source of truth, love, hope, and goodness,
things will get withered rather quickly. Without the life-giving
sap, the fruit is worthless. The strength of the branch fades due
to its ill-health on the inside. This we need to be careful to stay
connected. So what are the things that disconnect or dehydrate
us? I would like to place one more foundation stone at your feet
before we move on; look up and read Matthew 6:19-24.

What are the three main points?

1.

2.

3.

These three points are very important to who we are as Christians. When we fill up on the things of this world, we become separated from the vine and start to wither. If we are attached, we are in God's plan of how to live. We are doing what His Word tells us to do. We become His "attachment," His followers that seek to do His will. If I know God, I know His will, and I become a bearer of fruit.

What is it that you treasure?

In verse 19 (NIV), "Do not store up for yourselves treasures on earth, where moths and vermin destroy, and where thieves break in and steal." Here, the Greek is talking about the type of treasure that you amass or heap up. The kind of treasure that some pirate has tucked away in a cave or buried in the sand. Or the type that the Egyptian Pharaohs would gather and leave in a pyramid, only to have the grave robbers destroy and steal what belonged to someone who is no longer alive. The Greek text mentions another type of treasure in verse 21 (AMP), "For where your treasure is, there your heart will be also." This is referring to a treasure that you deposit and is of wealth. The treasures that the Lord is referring to are the ones we deposit in heaven.

I want you to do a head-to-toe assessment. Taking time to meditate is a very valuable way to assess where you are and what adjustments you need to make in your life. When Christians meditate, they don't say a mantra over and over. No, instead, you choose a Bible verse or concept that you know God is working on you to keep you healthy. Do you exhibit the sign and symptoms of a heart for Jesus? How is your relationship with Him? Think and contemplate in order to develop and fortify your soul and mind. Take time to really focus on the area of character building needed as a healthy Christian. We, in our culture, keep ourselves so busy that we have allowed our minds to get weak from lack of true thought and challenge.

So here are the areas for review and meditation:

1. Am I connected to the vine? Or is the gardener about to cut me out, and why?

2. What type of fruit do I bear, if any?

3. What do I treasure, and what should I be treasuring?

4. Am I dehydrated from the pursuit of treasures that rot and rust?

5. Does God have a hold of my whole heart?

6. Are my eyes healthy?

7. What darkness do I need to start illuminating?

8. Who do I serve?

9. What can I start doing to get healthy and rehydrate with the living water?

10. Did I take enough time to meditate for wisdom and insight?

Prayer

Dear Lord,

I want You as the Lord of my life, Master in everything. Help me to identify the things that dehydrate me and keep me unhealthy. I want to stay attached to the vine, so prune out of my life the things that are not of You. Help me to see the false treasures that are "Mammon" in my life. I am looking forward to the healthy and hydrated days that are mine to have as a true disciple! To be able to bear fruit as I am filled with Your joy and love. Amen.

> I rejoice in your word like one who discovers a great treasure.
>
> Psalm 119:162 (NLT)

The Treasure Hunt

What is a treasure? A treasure has value. That value came from the fact that you worked hard for it, or maybe you were fortunate to inherit something of great worth. Some things that you treasure may not be tangible, for example, the love of your family. A treasure may also have a certain amount of power over us. It can motivate, stimulate, and provoke people to pursue its rewards. Our energy becomes focused on achieving the possession of that treasured item. We can become obsessed with attaining it and the rewards that we perceive it offers. A treasure can be something that is good. Just remember that, like the "acorns of life," even too much of a good thing can make us out of balance. What you treasure can be on one extreme or the other. Make some more lists to help you see what it is that you treasure.

Earthly treasures, the things I have here and now:

Treasures in heaven, the fruit produced while I am here as a Christian:

So how did your lists shape up? Were you surprised at any of your answers? Back to Matthew 6:22 (NKJV), "The lamp of the body is the eye. Therefore if your eye is good, your whole body will be full of light." What a great verse! Our eyes are the portals to who we are. They are the gate or entrance to who we are as people. I know my eyes can get me in trouble or keep me correctly focused. We need to be good stewards of the things that we allow to pass through our eyes and into our hearts and minds. If we do not keep watch over our entertainment, desires, and lifestyle, we are going to dehydrate. We fill up on the wrong things, and a state of spiritual illness sets in quickly. In our culture today, we have so much of what we want but need to pay better attention to what we need. I don't know about you, but I do not want to remain in the darkness. I want the light to illuminate my heart! What are the items that a thief can steal? What cannot be taken from you?

> "No one can serve two masters. Either you will hate the one and love the other, or you will be devoted to the one and despise the other. You cannot serve both God and money."
>
> Matthew 6:24 (NIV)

Money, wealth, or mammon are descriptions of treasures that can master our decisions in life. "Mammon" is an interesting word; it means a sort of "false god" associated with wealth. In other words, there is a worship mindset associated with wealth. What does it mean to be wealthy? Trust me; if you are living in North America, you are wealthy in a global perspective. It is the accumulation of many possessions and money. We have so much that it can be difficult to keep track of our possessions. We have a good friend, Bob, who retired by building storage units for people who need more space for their treasures. Bob shares how amazed he is that people don't even know what they have because they have so much that they lose account of their belongings. It states that the renters will rent space for items of little to no value just to have a place to put them. Our society has had to pay the consequences of "Mammon" in the recent crisis of debt that has been accumulated. Some families have lost their homes because they have spent more than they earn.

When will we become satisfied?

When is enough enough?

WEEK FIVE

Distracted

Day Two

So just like horses, we are going to talk about our need to keep properly hydrated by the "living water." If we don't, we become dried up and dehydrated. For example, when I have been out in my vegetable garden working hard and sweating from some sort of strenuous activity, I will go into the house for some refreshment. I cross the back porch, open the door; as I pass by the water decanter, I open the refrigerator, and there is my jar of inviting iced coffee. I pour a tall glass, and then back out to the garden I go with a cool drink in my hand. I love to sit under my oak tree on my little bench and drink ice-cold coffee in the heat of the day. I love iced coffee in the summertime! I am very fond of sitting back and admiring my achievements and plan what needs to be done next. The coffee is usually strong with chocolate, a touch of cinnamon, slightly sweet with milk. Ah, the pleasure of gazing at the work I have done with a warm breeze on my face as I sit in the shade and sip on my coffee. The coffee gives me the needed energy that I want from the caffeine after working as hard as I have. It is so good that sometimes, I go back for a second tall glass.

Not!

What are you talking about? Yes, I have done that in the past, but I have learned over the years to be smart and take care of myself. Coffee is the worst thing to drink on a hot day when you have been sweating. The above coffee drink is only consumed if I have had more than enough of the adequate clean, pure water needed, then and only then, as a treat. Caffeine in coffee is actually a diuretic. It will pull the fluids that you have out of your system, thus increasing your state of dehydration rather than helping your fluid balance. Don't get me wrong, I do drink coffee, but I drink in balance with the freshwater that is good for me.

It is so easy to get distracted from what you are supposed to be doing. The above scenario happened to me, and a case of heat exhaustion followed. I was so distracted by the desire for sweet with a zip that I walked right past the water decanter and went for what I wanted, not what I needed. Don't we all do that at some point in our lives? We allow the distractions to veer us from the waters of life that we need.

What type of good or bad distractions do you face on a daily basis?

Are there distractions in your life today that are harmful to you?

To be distracted comes in many shapes and forms. Distraction can be in the form of entertainment that whisks us away from the daily drudge. Distraction can also take the form of a disturbance or a commotion that diverts our attention from what we were supposed to be doing. Or it can be in the form of lust for things that we don't really need and we just think we deserve.

The enemy is tricky; things are not always what they appear. For example, time spent catching up with friends on the Internet can go bad if we do not have the proper boundaries or filters set in place. I have heard too many sad stories recently of marriages breaking up as a result of pornography sites or chatrooms. Or how about an unexpected event, like a divorce or a financial crisis, to get you off track and dried up? We are going to look at examples that Jesus gives us regarding things in life that distract us from the life we should be living. Let's start with a woman named Martha. She was hosting Jesus and the disciples as they were traveling. Read Luke 10:38-42 in your Bible.

What are three things that you know about Martha from verses 38-40?

1.

2.

3.

Have you ever been too busy for relationship? I have and definitely regretted it when the opportunity to have a relationship with people had passed. One of the worst feelings is being in the kitchen at Christmas and missing out on all the laughter in the other room! I forget, sometimes, that it is the celebration of Jesus' birth, not about a meal. Remember Jesus is about relationship. I have never noticed in the Bible where it states, "And the food is why they gathered together."

Back to the simplicity of meeting together, remember the purpose of the event. Okay, now wait a minute, are you suggesting I serve fast food at Christmas for honored guests? No, I am reminding us of the distraction of the meal preparation from the chance to be with those that the Lord has in your life and the reason for the celebration. Can you recall a time when you were too busy for the Lord with something that you viewed as important? What was it that helped you to make a better choice on how your time was spent?

Write down that time recalled and how you improved your choices the next time.

So what about her sister, Mary? I love the picture painted of her sitting at Jesus' feet, listening. Her focus is correct; she has her priorities where they belong. Then, in the following two verses, Jesus responds in love (verses 41-42, NIV):

> "Martha, Martha," the Lord answered, "you are worried and upset about many things, but few things are needed— or indeed only one. Mary has chosen what is better, and it will not be taken away from her."

Oh, how I want to choose what is best for me.

Stop and think about the things in your life that you need to choose that are better and will not be taken away.

1.

2.

3.

4.

5.

I would have to venture to say that most of our worries are based upon distractions from the truth. If I am concerned about the way my life is going, I can lose sleep as I fret about what I should be doing. This is a disruption in my thoughts from the truth of God's love and concern for me. These dark thoughts will dry me up as I allow them to overtake the reality of who God is. Before we close today, I want to take a good look at Matthew 6:19-36. We looked at these verses yesterday, but I want to explore another facet of their detail. Please read Matthew 6:19-34 and then answer the following questions.

1. What are the characteristics of good eyes, and how do you keep them healthy?

2. What happens to us if our eyes become unhealthy and bad?

3. Tell me again, who are the two masters, and which one are we to serve?

4. What are we not to worry about?

5. Where are we to look for examples of God's provision?

6. God says "don't" what?

7. What should we seek?

8. So what about tomorrow and each day?

Prayer

Dear Lord,

I want to fill up on You and You alone. Help me to drink in Your words and wisdom with a healthy thirst for more and more. Forgive me for the distractions that keep me from the truth of who You are. Help me to keep my eyes on You and to choose what is best for me. Help me not to waste my time fretting about things that are not in my control but are under your care where they belong. Amen.

Stepping Out

Day Three

Now, let us look to one of my favorite disciples, Peter. I like Peter; I appreciate his willingness to step out. I have a saying for myself that goes like this, "I jump in the water and then wonder why I am wet." Meaning I don't always think before I act. Peter was a fisherman, bold in his actions and passionate about all he did. We see an example of this after the feeding of the five thousand. Jesus gives instructions to the disciples to go, and they obey.

> Immediately Jesus told his followers to get into the boat and go ahead of him across the lake. He stayed there to send the people home. After he had sent them away, he went by himself up into the hills to pray. It was late, and Jesus was there alone. By this time, the boat was already far away from land. It was being hit by waves, because the wind was blowing against it. Between three and six o'clock in the morning, Jesus came to them, walking on the water. When his followers saw him walking on the water, they were afraid. They said, "It's a ghost!" and cried out in fear. But Jesus quickly spoke to them, "Have courage! It is I. Do not be afraid." Peter said, "Lord, if it is really you, then command me to come to you on the water." Jesus said, "Come." And Peter left the boat and walked on the water to Jesus. But when Peter saw the wind and the waves, he became afraid and began to sink. He shouted, "Lord, save me!"

Immediately Jesus reached out his hand and caught Peter. Jesus said, "Your faith is small. Why did you doubt?" After they got into the boat, the wind became calm. Then those who were in the boat worshiped Jesus and said, "Truly you are the Son of God!"

Matthew 14:22-33 (NCV)

I think that Peter was definitely distracted by the fearful uncertainty of the rough waves surrounding him. This fear had manifested itself into doubt. I want you to imagine for a moment that you are the one in the boat. Jesus has just appeared out of the inky darkness amidst the storm that rages around you but wait, Jesus calls to those in the boat.

1. Are there any storms in your life today? Can you describe what they are? If not, can you recall some storm of the past that instilled fear into your heart?

2. What does Jesus tell those who are in the boat?

3. What does it mean to you to have courage?

Then Peter responds with a request, "Lord, if it is really you, then command me to come to you on the water." But why would he even want to leave the safety of the boat? If he was to remain, chances are that he would stay afloat, stay just where he has always been, a fisherman in a boat on a stormy lake. Although on the other hand, his Lord is saying, "Come, Peter, step out of what you know, the storm that surrounds you, and come."

4. Can you hear the Lord beckoning you to step out of the boat?

5. Are you taking that step out of the boat? Why or why not?

The boat could represent the way things are and have been. The storm could be the distractions and doubts that want to knock you off balance. Once again, Jesus is trying to help and encourage someone who is overwhelmed by the wind-blown waves. For the woman at the well, it was separation from her community, a lifestyle of shame and confusion of who God really was. For Peter, it is the fear of the present circumstances of a sea-tossed boat. So over the side climbs Peter, bold as ever, acting out in a desire to be near his Lord. Can you imagine what that must have been like? Close your eyes and envision the encounter, "And Peter left the boat and walked on the water to Jesus."

6. Describe what you think those first steps might have felt like:

7. What do the "turbulent waters" represent to you?

For me, it would have been beyond words, a glorious moment of invincibility. To have Jesus locked in focus and moving across the lake and its unstable water under my feet. Wow! Peter is a man of faith! *What are you saying, Caprice? He sank.* Yes, but he had the courage to step out of the boat in the direction of the Lord. Please make a list of adjectives that might describe that moment of faith.

8. My list of faith adjectives:

Oh, how many times have we been defeated in our moments of triumph? I do not know about you, but I do understand doubt. To be uncertain about your current affairs due to the disappointment of promises unfulfilled. To have hope crushed the very moment it took root in your heart and mind. To see the trust that you had in someone or something drown in the sea of despair. "But when Peter saw the wind and the waves, he became afraid and began to sink."

But here is the good news as we read the next statement, "He shouted, 'Lord, save me!'" This is why I love Peter's example. He didn't clear his throat and say, "Excuse me, Jesus, I think things are not going as planned, gulp, gulp. The water is getting a little deep, gulp, gulp. Oh well, don't bother about poor little me; I will just try to swim back to the boat; I was wrong to even ask." No, Peter shouted, "Lord, save me!" "Immediately, Jesus reached out his hand and caught Peter."

9. What are the cries for help that you need to shout to the Lord?

Imagine that, like the woman at the well, you are alone with Jesus. It is the Lord of the living water who is offering you the water that satisfies. You, too, have become dried up from doubt, but the Lord is reaching out to grab your hand. Asking you not to look at the things that are troubling you, to trust in His ability to get you through the turbulent waters. What is it that keeps you from taking a hold of the Master's hand?

Then come the words, "Your faith is small. Why did you doubt?" Ouch! We heard this yesterday too, "Don't have so little faith!" in response to worry about what to eat or to wear. All I can say is that I don't want my faith to remain insignificant or of no consequence. I want a faith that will deliver me through the cold storms that rant and rave in this life, don't you?

So how do you go from little faith to BIG FAITH?

1. One of the places that *big faith* comes from is the vine. You need to be tapped into the source in order to bear good fruit versus fruit that is rotten. The fruit of the vine yields faith. If you are connected, you will develop good fruit.

2. The gifts of the Spirit that will remain are faith, hope, and love. So out of the three that remain, one of them is faith. Faith is

a valuable and everlasting gift from the Holy Spirit. We cannot do anything to earn it.

3. Faith is putting God's love into action.

4. Hebrews 11:1 (NLT), "Faith is the confidence that what we hope for will actually happen; it gives us assurance about things we cannot see."

Hebrews 11:6 (NASB), "And without faith it is impossible to please Him, for he who comes to God must believe that He is and that He is a rewarder of those who seek Him."

5. Matthew 17:20-21 (NLT), "'You don't have enough faith,' Jesus told them. 'I tell you the truth, if you had faith even as small as a mustard seed, you could say to this mountain, "Move from here to there," and it would move. Nothing would be impossible.'"

Consider the clay water jar that the woman of the well had. She was filling it with the items of this world that would not sustain her through the storms of life. You, too, have a jar of clay. Jesus talks about this jar in 2 Corinthians 4:5-9 (NIV):

> For what we preach is not ourselves, but Jesus Christ as Lord, and ourselves as your servants for Jesus' sake. For God, who said, "Let light shine out of darkness," made his light shine in our hearts to give us the light of the knowledge of God's glory displayed in the face of Christ. But we have this treasure in jars of clay to show that this all-surpassing power is from God and not from us. We are hard pressed on every side, but not crushed; perplexed, but not in despair; persecuted, but not abandoned; struck down, but not destroyed.

In the times of Jesus, people did not have secure banks to store their valuables. So they would hide them in everyday clay jars that had an ordinary appearance. When a thief was searching for something to steal, they would pass by the "everyday" clay jar, yet hidden inside was a priceless treasure. The clay jars represent us (the ordinary vessel) with the treasure of Jesus (the priceless treasure) in our hearts. Our little seed of faith grows and grows with the trust and hope that we have in the Lord as Savior. We choose, over time, to fill our jars with the living water, and the fuller they get, the less room there is for the doubts, distractions, and fears of this world.

Prayer

Lord,

I want *big faith*! I want to fill my jar with Your treasures that come from reading Your Word, stepping out of the boat, and knowing that You are God. Help me to grab a hold of Your hand and not to lose sight of who You are in the storms that rage around me. Thank You for loving me even in my little faith days. Amen.

Additional Reading

Take the time to read Hebrews chapter 11. It is God's hallmark of faith.

Disappointment

Day Four

Horses have a strong herding instinct. So much so that if you separate them from what or whom they perceive as their herd, they can become very distressed. We have a very good Christian friend who is a professional roper. David shares his talents and love of horses with others. He belongs to a group called the Fellowship of Christian Cowboys. The group travels around to arenas where riders gather on Sundays to practice and compete in roping, to share the Word of God to anyone who will listen, and fellowship with other believers. David also takes a week every summer to help staff Rodeo Bible Camp for youth. One year, they were in Firebaugh, CA, and it should have been called fireball due to the sweltering temperatures that week. David had put his roping horse in a corral away from the other horses to give her a rest. This instilled a sense of fear in his beloved roping horse due to the unfamiliar surroundings and solitude. His horse started to pace and fret, refused to drink, and took a sudden turn for the worst. Fortunately, David was there to care for his horse and administer to her needs. He brought his mare back to her trailer, which was a place of familiarity. He hosed her off with some tepid water and soothed her with a calm voice and gentle strokes of his hand. The security of knowing her master was there composed her; she settled down and soon began to drink water.

The disciple Peter had the nerve to walk on water. It took courage to step out of the boat onto the rough waves. He did not sink until the whirling sea of troubles around him distracted him, and he began to doubt. It was his Master's care that saved him that day from drowning. Just like my friend David recognized the need of his horse to be reconnected with the one who cared about her, Jesus knows that we need to be connected to Him in times of stress.

Peter was a disciple. Have you ever wanted to belong to an organization or group? Have you wanted to associate with someone or something that shares a common interest or a purpose? Most of us can identify with the fact that at some time in our lives, we have wanted to belong to something. It usually roots itself in a similar goal shared by the other members, for example, a club, family, or circle of friends. In a sense, we want to know that there are other people out there who are like us. It gives us a feeling of security to know we are not alone.

Peter belonged to a group of people who sat under the teaching of a progressive and controversial rabbi. That rabbi-teacher was Jesus. He ruffled many feathers because of His teachings. One of the group members had decided it was time to change course and join the other side. None of the other disciples knew that something was brewing and that one of them was planning on leaving the group.

> Then one of the twelve, named Judas Iscariot, went to the chief priests and said, "What are you willing to give me to betray Him to you?" And they weighed out thirty pieces of silver to him. From then on he began looking for a good opportunity to betray Jesus.
> Matthew 26:14-16 (NASB)

Not only is he leaving the group of disciples, but he is also entering the enemy's camp. The seed of deceit has been planted.

We have established that we need to "know God." But do you know who you are and what defines who you are? Is it your family, your job, your hobbies, your political affiliation, your own opinion, or someone else's? If you were to answer the question "who are you?" How would you define the answer? Please explain.

1. So, who are you?

2. What do you believe and stand for?

3. What groups do you belong to, if any?

4. Have you ever been betrayed? Describe what it felt like.

God created us to have fellowship with other people, to bond, connect, and to live in community. When we become disconnected, loss settles into our thoughts, and we can develop the fear of separation.

5. Have you ever suffered a loss from your source or connection?

6. What if the source of your bonding becomes unpopular or in danger of persecution? Will you stand firm, defend, run, disown, or reject?

The things that empty and dehydrate us can come from those who we think are very close to us. The "kiss of betrayal" can rip at the heart of who we are and impact our reactions to others. A gaping heart wound, if not dealt with, can scab over into hate, isolation, withdrawal, and despair. If it continues to progress, we can even develop scar tissue. Scar tissue is hard, impermeable tissue that is tough and unyielding. In order to restore this wound, we need a touch from the master physician and healer. Jesus, after having washed His disciples' feet in a humble display of love and service, says, "I tell you the truth, slaves are not greater than their master. Nor is the messenger more important than the one who sends the message. Now that you know these things, God will bless you for doing them" (John 13:16-17, NLT).

He is setting the stage for equality among people; no longer will there be room for status among those who believe. No one person is of greater worth than the other. Then, this most inconceivable declaration is poured out before us; John 13:21 (NLT) states, "Now Jesus was deeply troubled, and he exclaimed, 'I tell you the truth, one of you will betray me!'"

Did you catch that? Jesus is saddened and deeply distressed. He is going to be betrayed. Have you ever had the foreknowledge that someone who was close to you was not who you thought they were?

7. Take the time to reflect back to that realization. What was it like?

8. Did this result in a change of life as you knew it? What changes occurred?

Let me ask you one more searching question. Have you ever been the betrayer? Take a moment and allow the Holy Spirit to speak to you and reveal any betrayals that might be of your doing. If so, Jesus forgives and restores all who ask. Ask for forgiveness right now.

Jesus, help me to restore my life to where it should be as Your vessel, ready to pour out Your love for others. The only way I can pour out Your love is to be sure that it is full of Your fruit and clean from sin.

Lord, please forgive me for betraying _____.

Or, Lord please help me to forgive _____ for betraying me.

Jesus then states something profound in verses 34-35 (MSG):

"Let me give you a new command: Love one another. In the same way I loved you, you love one another. This is how everyone will recognize that you are my disciples — when they see the love you have for each other."

In the midst of chaotic betrayal, Jesus is telling His disciples to love as He loves. A new command is given as the only solution to heal the deep wound that betrayal leaves. We need to take courage in the fact that Jesus knows exactly how it felt. If you have experienced the "kiss of betrayal," you need to give it over to the Lord for repair as only He can restore. He understands; He cares about your grief from carrying such a burden. The Lord wants us to fill up so full of His love that we overflow into the lives of others and the situations around us. His love is pure and true, and we need to stuff our hearts and water jars so full that nothing else can fit in. Do not be tempted to fill up with the sorrows of the past. Do not grab a handful of the dirty lies of the enemy. We do not want to leave room for anything that might parch and dry up who we were created to be. When times get tough, we need to drink up the word, be in prayer and surround ourselves with other strong believers.

My friend David is his horse's caregiver. He provides for and protects her. No matter how strong David's concern is for his horse, it is pale in comparison to God's love for us. No matter how horrifying your betrayal may have been. How sorrowful the separation from those you thought you were connected to forever. God is the true source of love. He is the vine that sustains and supports. He is the only eternal love.

Prayer

Oh Father God,

I thank You for the gift of Your Son Jesus. I am so grateful that I can turn to Your Word to understand that I am not alone in any trial that surrounds me today, yesterday, or tomorrow. You care for me, love me, and I am forever connected to You. If someone in this world betrays me, I know that You love me, and Your love can pour out of me into my situations and heal the deepest of wounds. Thank You. Thank You, Lord of my life! Amen.

Hard Pressed

Day Five

Stress can cause us to become anxious and emotionally overwhelmed. We can develop physical symptoms like sweaty palms, dry mouth, elevated blood pressure, pounding heart, and maybe even depression. Remember that in order to be in balance, we need a sense of stability. If our lives and the world around us are out of control, just like the horse, we can become dehydrated from too much strain and not enough filling up on the living waters.

Peter had some real trials during the final days of Jesus' ministry. I would have to say that I would have been very stressed at the events taking place in Judea. The Roman officials were threatened by Jesus and the movement that was growing. Rumors of Jesus' arrest were on the lips of many, and the fear of being associated with His ministry and possible arrest cooled the enthusiasm of several. Jesus was preparing His disciples for His crucifixion by spending some time with them sharing the Passover meal.

> Jesus sent Peter and John, saying, "Go and make preparations for us to eat the Passover." "Where do you want us to prepare for it?" they asked. He replied, "As you enter the city, a man carrying a jar of water will meet you. Follow him to the house that he enters, and say to the owner of the house, 'The Teacher asks: Where is the guest room, where I may eat the Passover

with my disciples?' He will show you a large room upstairs, all furnished. Make preparations there." They left and found things just as Jesus had told them. So they prepared the Passover.

Luke 22:8-13 (NIV)

Events are making it tougher to meet together; Jesus knows that time is fleeting. As Jesus' short ministry of three years is drawing to a close, His students are having a hard time understanding the meaning of some of His lessons. As the events of that evening continue, they sing a hymn and leave the upper room to go to the Mount of Olives. As they are walking, Jesus predicts Peter's denial:

> On the way, Jesus told them, "All of you will desert me. For the Scriptures say, 'God will strike the Shepherd, and the sheep will be scattered.' But after I am raised from the dead, I will go ahead of you to Galilee and meet you there." Peter said to him, "Even if everyone else deserts you, I never will." Jesus replied, "I tell you the truth, Peter—this very night, before the rooster crows twice, you will deny three times that you even know me." "No!" Peter declared emphatically. "Even if I have to die with you, I will never deny you!" And all the others vowed the same.
>
> Mark 14:27-31 (NLT

"God will strike the Shepherd, and the sheep will be scattered." Sheep are "follow the leader" type of animals and, in some ways, so docile that they can be rather stupid. That is why they need a shepherd; they require a good keeper of the flock. Some have heard believers referred to as sheep, and trust me; this is not always a compliment. If their shepherd goes missing and a predator shows up, they will take off in any direction possible. This leaves sheep very vulnerable because they do not possess sharp teeth, claws, or a keen mind; thus, they have no means of defense.

Have you ever been scattered due to a leader who was removed from your life for one reason or another? That leader could have been a father, husband, teacher, or pastor. It would have been someone who you looked to for direction and protection.

What were some of your reactions and emotions?

As the evening progresses, Jesus is betrayed.:

> And He came out and proceeded as was His custom to the Mount of Olives; and the disciples also followed Him. When He arrived at the place, He said to them, "Pray that you may not enter into temptation." And He withdrew from them about a stone's throw, and He knelt down and began to pray, saying, "Father, if You are willing, remove this cup from Me; yet not My will, but Yours be done." Now an angel from heaven appeared to Him, strengthening Him. And being in agony He was praying very fervently; and His sweat became like drops of blood, falling down upon the ground.
>
> Luke 22:39-44 (NASB)

1. What does Jesus tell His disciples to do so that they will not fall into temptation?

2. Jesus asks His Father to _____ but yields to God's

_____.

3. In His anguish, He is strengthened by an _____ .

Verses 45-46 (NCV), "When he finished praying, he went to his followers and found them asleep because of their sadness. Jesus said to them, 'Why are you sleeping? Get up and pray for strength against temptation.'" The type of exhausted sorrow is full of heaviness and grief.

4. Jesus tells them to pray again because they are _____ and to prevent them from _____.

5. What do you do to keep you strong when feeling overwhelmed and temptation is pulling at you to abandon what is good and right?

Then, the unthinkable happens. Verses 47-48 (NIV), "While he was still speaking a crowd came up, and the man who was called Judas, one of the Twelve, was leading them. He approached Jesus to kiss him, but Jesus asked him, 'Judas, are you betraying the Son of Man with a kiss?'"

6. We talked about this betrayal yesterday. It is truly an awful experience. Do you have any other thoughts about betrayal?

7. The betrayer's kiss. What would be going through your mind as you realized that someone that you thought was one of your team had revealed Jesus to the enemy?

8. Lack of trust due to disappointment is a very scorching mindset. It burns so intensely that it affects how we react to others. It shrivels our hearts until we can learn to forgive and love like Jesus. Share a story of overcoming disappointment.

The chief priest, temple guard, and the elders take Jesus to the high priest for questioning. This was a Jewish trial held in the cloak of darkness.

> Simon Peter followed Jesus, as did another of the disciples. That other disciple was acquainted with the high priest, so he was allowed to enter the high priest's courtyard with Jesus. Peter had to stay outside the gate. Then the disciple who knew the high priest spoke to the woman watching at the gate, and she let Peter in. The woman asked Peter, "You're not one of that man's disciples, are you?" "No," he said, "I am not." Because it was cold, the household servants and the guards had made a charcoal fire. They stood around it, warming themselves, and Peter stood with them, warming himself. Inside, the high priest began asking Jesus about his followers and what he had been teaching them.
>
> John 18:15-19 (NLT)

Peter was bold, and again, he showed courage to even follow the Jewish leaders to their trial. I am sure that he was gripped with the fear of imprisonment as he was asked at the gate if he was a disciple. The shadows of the night danced across his face as he warmed himself by the small fire. I wonder if he thought that no one would notice him, but he is questioned again. I think I would have been panicked by then. To my shame, I admit to you that I have not always been bold about my relationship with Jesus. Have you? When I first became a Christian, I had friends who I thought the world of, and it mattered to me that I fit in. I tried subtle ways to blend into the group. When I was with my friends who were not Christians, I spoke, dressed, and acted like them. Where they went, I went; what they did, I did. I denied

Jesus by my actions and associations. I definitely did not stand out in a crowd of unbelievers; there was no reflection of Jesus in my eyes.

9. When did you first understand the call of the Spirit to a change of character, a quality of personality that was a true reflection of Jesus?

10. Was it difficult for you to pull yourself from who you used to be? Describe what that transition was like.

11. Look up 2 Corinthians 5:17 and rewrite it in your own words.

Peter disowns Jesus in Luke 22:59-62 (NIV):

> About an hour later another asserted, "Certainly this fellow was with him, for he is a Galilean." Peter replied, "Man, I don't know what you're talking about!" Just as he was speaking, the rooster crowed. The Lord turned and looked straight at Peter. Then Peter remembered the word the Lord had spoken to him: "Before the rooster crows today, you will disown me three times." And he went outside and wept bitterly.

The Lord looked straight at Peter. Oh my, I think I would have melted. Could you imagine how He must have felt? These are the same eyes that beckoned Him to step out of the boat. I guess Peter had found comfort inside the safety of the boat of denial this time.

12. Have you ever wept bitterly in remorse over your actions? Could you share what the remorse that you felt was like?

I close again this week with 2 Corinthians 4:8-10 (NIV):

> We are hard pressed on every side, but not crushed; perplexed, but not in despair; persecuted, but not abandoned; struck down, but not destroyed. We always carry around in our body the death of Jesus, so that the life of Jesus may also be revealed in our body.

Write your own prayer in the space below.

My prayer

WEEK SIX

The Horse and the Rider

Over these last six weeks, we have talked about connecting. The woman at the well struggled with this connection at first. But once she grabbed a hold, she was off and running, leaving her water jar of the world behind. Then, we spoke about what it was to be empty and the living water that satisfies, not the acorns of this world. Then, we leaned on our well of understanding and looked deep into the question, "How do you know that you know God?" Do we know the "BIG G" God or the god of the "little g"? This was an important question to ask ourselves. Then, we discovered contrasts and who was knocking at our hearts. Then last week, we did our head-to-toe, inside-and-out assessments.

I would like to make a shift in perspective for the introduction to our last week together. I want you to take the viewpoint of the rider as our Master, and guess what that makes you and me? You are correct, the horse! When you ride, there is this relationship between the horse and rider that can be fully engaged. A relationship of one heart and mind that translates into action. Action because time spent training a horse to develop sensitivity to command signals equals a desired response.

A horse is trained to move away from stimulus; for example, I put pressure from my right heel into the horse's side, and the horse will veer to the left. If I pull back on the reins, the horse will want to stop in order to move away from the pulling of the bit in its mouth. When sitting in the saddle, a slight adjustment of weight can alter the direction of the horse; by leaning on my left hip, the horse will move to the right. Every shift in the saddle is translated to the horse as a cue to move. The reason the horse follows through with these moves is because of repetitious training and experience that is reinforced for a desired result. This develops to a level of connection in which my thoughts result in my action, which gives the horse a learned response of movement. This is what you see in some amazing performances of equestrian events. The unified precision of horse and rider is a spectacular sight to behold.

I can still remember the first time I fully connected with my horse, Sundance. We were up in the hills on a trail that we had ridden numerous times before, but never with the unity that we had on that day. It was as if his four hooves were my two feet. I had that situational awareness of where we both were on that trail. We rode together at a canter up and down the narrow trail. As I saw a downed limp ahead of us, in my mind, we jumped, and before I knew it, we were airborne and clearing the obstacle. I did not have time to think; I just prepared myself for the jump. This cued my horse, and over we went. I had the confidence that Sundance had the ability to follow through. It was truly amazing to be one with God's creation. The motion of unity is very difficult to describe and spectacular to experience!

This is what God wants from us. As the horse anticipates its master's moves, we, too, need to be alert to our Master's calling for action. Over these last five weeks, we have talked about connecting. The woman at the well struggled with this connection at first. But once she grabbed a hold, she was off and running, leaving her water jar of the world behind. Then, we spoke about what it was to be empty and the living water that satisfies, not the acorns of this world. Then, we leaned on our well of understanding and looked deep into the question, "How do you know that you know God?" Do we know the "BIG G" God or the god of the "little g"? This was an important question to ask ourselves. Then, we discovered contrasts and who was knocking at our hearts. Then last week, we did our head-to-toe, inside-and-out assessments. All of these things have prepared us to be on cue for the Master's touch. That no matter how big the fallen limb is, we are ready and willing to take that leap of faith and move forward for God's call to serve.

So our last week is going to take on a final trail ride together as we walk together as believers. We will tether ourselves to John chapter four and the woman at the well. Just like she was willing to connect to our Lord Jesus, we too must connect to continue on the trail and don't be left in the barn.

My Heart Is Smiling

Day One

Avery was an incredible instructor and encourager to our daughters as they developed their skills in preparation for competition. She taught them with kind patience; she didn't skip any of the necessary details, expected commitment, and gave them her needed support. The girls respected Avery's instruction and wanted to succeed as horsemen. They would practice their skills until they were refined in the saddle. They sought to do well at their task and to please her. The reward of the tedious hours was a blue ribbon, a golden trophy, or best yet, the wonder words, "Job well done!"

Can you recall a time that you had the contentment of knowing that you had done a great job? A task was completed, and now you could sit back and ponder the satisfaction of a job well done.

Fulfillment and satisfaction come from many sources. In the Sermon on the Mount, Jesus is speaking to those who are looking for answers to the burning questions in their hearts and minds. The Lord hit the nail on the head with His amazing words. In Matthew 5:6 (ESV), Jesus states:

> "Blessed are those who hunger and thirst for righteousness, for they shall be satisfied."

1. So what does it mean to hunger and thirst for righteousness?

2. Why do you think that this thirsting will satisfy?

Jesus told a parable of a master who entrusted his servants with money (talents) while he was gone. When the master returns, he tells two of his servants in Matthew 25:23 (AMP):

> His master said to him, "Well done, you upright [honorable, admirable] and faithful servant! You have been faithful and trustworthy over a little; I will put you in charge of much. Enter into and share the joy [the delight, the blessedness] which your master enjoys."

Oh, how I long to hear those words from Jesus when I get to heaven. I want to have the pleasure of knowing that I have served well.

3. What do you think being a faithful servant means?

4. Jesus is letting us know in this parable that if we are faithful in a _____ thing, He will put us in charge of _____ things.

5. What do you think the "things" are?

To share in the happiness of my Master! When one of my daughters would win a blue ribbon, Avery and my daughter shared a personal pleasure. It was personal because of the intimate relationship that they had developed in the process of commitment to their goal. We, too, share a personal delight with the Lord when we have completed a task or have learned from a new opportunity.

Please read in your Bible Matthew 25:14-30.

Let the words to the lazy servant sink in. It is worthy to note that the talents are the ability or gift from the master; they are to be used and multiplied because of their value and purpose for the master. The principle is that of money that earns interest or increases with use. When we are truly full of happiness and delight from our relationship with our master, it increases to the point of overflowing.

6. What did you think about the master's response to the "lazy servant"?

I love what the psalmist says about delighting in the Lord in Psalm 37:1-6 (NIV):

> Do not fret because of those who are evil
> or be envious of those who do wrong;
> for like the grass they will soon wither,
> like green plants they will soon die away.
> Trust in the LORD and do good;
> dwell in the land and enjoy safe pasture.
> Take delight in the LORD,
> and he will give you the desires of your heart.
> Commit your way to the LORD;
> trust in him and he will do this:
> He will make your righteous reward shine like the dawn,
> your vindication like the noonday sun.

Here we see three amazing points:

1. Trust in the Lord and do good.

2. Enjoy the safety where you are and dwell in the land.

3. Delight in the Lord, and He will give you the desires of your heart.

The faith and belief that what God would have us do is good for us and excellent for those we serve. If we stay where we are placed and settle in to serve, we will find happiness in the job we do. And here is the blue ribbon; He will give you the desires of your heart. Why? Because we are living according to God's will and plan for our lives.

7. Can you describe a time that you received the desire of your heart as a result of your delight in the Lord as you pursued His righteousness?

I will boast only in the Lord; let all who are helpless take heart. Come, let us tell of the Lord's greatness; let us exalt his name together.

Psalm 34:2-3 (NLT)

8. Praise God for His greatness! Can you describe a time when it was difficult to trust in the Lord and do good, but you delighted in the fact that you ended well?

I prayed to the Lord, and he answered me. He freed me from all my fears. Those who look to him for help will be radiant with joy; no shadow of shame will darken their faces.

Psalm 34:4-5 (NLT)

9. What did the Lord free David from?

10. If we look to the Lord for help, what will be the result?

In my desperation I prayed, and the Lord listened; he saved me from all my troubles. For the angel of the Lord is a guard; he surrounds and defends all who fear him.

Psalm 34:6-7 (NLT)

Again, the answer comes because of prayer, distressed prayer. A prayer that cries out for an answer. The answer comes from the Lord, as He is our Savior from our troubles. He even provides protection for those He loves! He envelops and defends us in our time of greatest need. Why? Because we call on our Lord, the One who answers our prayers.

What is it that is troubling you?

Do you fear, or are you distressed about something?

Would you like to lay claim to the Lord as your "radiant joy"?

Take a minute and write a prayer that you would like answered:

My Prayer

Then, here is what you should do next. Psalm 34:8-10 (NLT):

> Taste and see that the Lord is good.
> Oh, the joys of those who take refuge in him!
> Fear the Lord, you his godly people,
> for those who fear him will have all they need.
> Even strong young lions sometimes go hungry,
> but those who trust in the Lord will lack no good thing.

Rewrite the two verses from above in a way that directly applies to you today:

I have this saying that "My heart is smiling." It smiles with joy, radiant joy that comes from the Lord! There are times that I can't do anything else but sing out to the Lord with a heart so full of love for Him and the things He has done in my life. God's love, not human love, is what the Greek calls agape.

> And so faith, hope, love abide [faith—conviction and belief respecting man's relation to God and divine things; hope—joyful and confident expectation of eternal salvation; love—true affection for God and man, growing out of God's love for and in us], these three; but the greatest of these is love.
> First Corinthians 13:13 (AMP)

My heart smiles because of the incredible experience of knowing God and His goodness. I have understood and witnessed that the Lord is good. This knowledge leads to a desire for more and more. I know that it is best to trust Him in the storms of life. I will climb out of the boat, no matter how great the effort or difficult the strain of the struggle, and grab a hold of the Lord's hand for shelter from the storm. To trust in Him yields a fulfillment that satisfies. It keeps me going back to the well to draw the living water and keep my jar full of the things that sustain, not the things of this world. Praise God in a song to Him for the Good that He has accomplished in you!

My Praise

WEEK SIX

Hand in Hand

Day Two

Have you ever wanted something so deeply that you thought and dreamed about it all the time? Have you ever hoped that the chance for something so desired would come true? Around our house, if you wanted something, your desire would develop into the confidence that you could attain it. If you wanted something bad enough, hard work and tenacity not to give up could yield the desired outcome. One of my daughters hoped to purchase and own a horse. This young lady was determined to make that dream come true.

My daughter worked around the house and ranch doing chores to earn the purchase price and title of "responsible." She was required to earn half the amount of the purchase price, the important fact being the commitment to the project. Was she willing to work for what she wanted? This was a question that needed to be answered by action, not words. Mama was certainly not going to take care of her horse. Time proved the desire of my daughter's heart to be true and genuine. So off Avery went with my girls and me on another adventure of the pursuit for the perfect horse.

Tasha was a beautiful solid black mare. The dream horse that only comes once in a lifetime. Sweet, gentle, well trained, and a lot of heart! Tasha was so unique that my daughter was actually the one having to be promoted for purchase. The woman selling

Tasha had to sell her "best friend" and was not going to sell her to just anyone. We, as a family, had to win this woman's approval for purchase. She even visited our ranch before she made her decision. The woman watched how my daughter approached and spoke to Tasha. How did she handle the mare in the arena? Did my daughter show any evidence of knowledge about horses? Avery's training had paid off, many came to look at Tasha, but it was this determined ten-year-old that had what it took and put her hope into action. Her desire to own a horse gave this young girl the satisfaction of owning Tasha, an incredible dream come true.

Faith and hope go hand in hand in the life of a believer. In Hebrews 11:1 (NKJV), it says, "Now faith is the substance of things hoped for, the evidence of things not seen." Have you ever hoped for something to happen in your future that almost felt impossible? Something so big that the vision of it appeared intangible?

What is it that you hope for? List three things that you hope will develop in the next year:

1.

2.

3.

A good example of the tenacity of hope that produces result is found in 1 Thessalonians 1:2-3 (NIV):

> We always thank God for all of you and continually mention you in our prayers. We remember before our God and Father your work produced by faith, your labor prompted by love, and your endurance inspired by hope in our Lord Jesus Christ.

The four main points of these two verses:

    a. We should be continually in _____ .

    b. The work that we do is a product of our _____ .

    c. Prompted by love, we_____ towards our goal.

    d. Endurance is inspired by _____.

This faith that we have is a result of the experience of what we have not seen. Because we have experienced the result of what we hoped could be acquired, we work towards its fulfillment. One of the experiences that we participate in is connecting with God through prayer. I have the privilege of talking with God, not talking to God. Did you catch that? Too many of us talk to God in a one-way conversation. Prayer is two-way communication with our Father. How far do you think my daughter would have gotten in a one-way conversation?

Back to the woman at the well and her conversation with Jesus, John 4:10 (ESV) says, "Jesus answered her, 'If you knew the gift of God, and who it is that is saying to you, "Give me a drink," you would have asked him, and he would have given you living water.'" The woman at the well asked a question, and Jesus answered her!

Here is another example in Ephesians 1:18-23 (NLT):

> I pray that your hearts will be flooded with light so
> that you can understand the confident hope he has
> given to those he called —his holy people who are his
> rich and glorious inheritance. I also pray that you will
> understand the incredible greatness of God's power for
> us who believe him. This is the same mighty power that
> raised Christ from the dead and seated him in the place
> of honor at God's right hand in the heavenly realms.
> Now he is far above any ruler or authority or power
> or leader or anything else—not only in this world but
> also in the world to come. God has put all things under
> the authority of Christ and has made him head over all
> things for the benefit of the church. And the church is
> his body; it is made full and complete by Christ, who
> fills all things everywhere with himself.

3. In Ephesians, what are some of the things that we are to
glean from this passage? Please make a list of at least five jewels
to be gleaned:

Hope... Do you ever hope for things that seem impossible? So big that you might not be able to attain them? For example, by myself, I cannot attain eternal life. My expectation for eternal life comes through the hope given to me by God through the gift of His Son Jesus. If I have the faith to believe in what I have not seen, I will receive the adoption into the family of God by accepting Jesus into my heart as my Savior. This adoption entitles me to the privileges of living forever with God in heaven.

What about hope for what seems without a solution? Can we find a hope that sustains us through the impossible? Things felt impossible for Mary, the mother of Jesus, in Luke 1:34-37 (NASB):

> Mary said to the angel, "How can this be, since I am a virgin?" The angel answered and said to her, "The Holy Spirit will come upon you, and the power of the Most High will overshadow you; and for that reason the holy Child shall be called the Son of God. And behold, even your relative Elizabeth has also conceived a son in her old age; and she who was called barren is now in her sixth month. For nothing will be impossible with God."

Here are two examples of answered hope. Mary is confused about the promises made to her and Elizabeth. The most encouraging answer from the angel is, "For nothing will be impossible with God." We need to be confident in this answer. Nothing, no-thing is impossible for God. This is hope defined for my heart that my God is capable of "any-thing" because He can do it all according to His will and care for me.

> Jesus looked at them and said, "For people this is impossible, but for God all things are possible."
> Matthew 19:26 (NCV)

Again, Jesus is speaking to His disciples about heaven and the gift of salvation. We have, as God's created, this innate desire to be in peace with God. Jeremiah 32:17 (NASB):

> Ah Lord God! Behold, You have made the heavens and the earth by Your great power and by Your outstretched arm! Nothing is too difficult for You.

3. When I think of outstretched arms, I am reminded of those that were stretched out for me on the cross. So what are the "impossible things" that you face today?

I want to end with this beautiful picture story of a tree that is growing by a constant stream of water. It does not need to look to any other source for its hope. All it needs to do is to send its roots deep into the ground where it is planted. Because of this constant source, it need not fear the trials that come. And the jewel in this is that it is a fruit-bearing tree.

> Blessed is the man who trusts in the LORD, whose trust is the LORD. He is like a tree planted by water, that sends out its roots by the stream, and does not fear when heat comes, for its leaves remain green, and is not anxious in the year of drought, for it does not cease to bear fruit.
>
> Jeremiah 17:7-8 (ESV)

Prayer:

Dear sweet Lord,

My hope is in You! I know that my lists from today are in Your hands, ready to be answered because You care for me, and "nothing" is impossible for You! I will trust in You, and I am grateful for Your promise that I am blessed because of this trust. In Your Son's precious name. Amen.

WEEK SIX

Side by Side
Day Three

Our ranch is rather large, with 288 plus or minus acres. That is how they sold it to us and how we bought it. The old-timers used to put a fence here and mark a pasture there. The land is situated in a coastal valley with ravines that have several creek beds. There are many trees of different types and a good-sized pond that a lot of people refer to as a small lake. From the top of our mountain, we take in some of the most amazing views of Mendocino County all the way to Napa in the east and Sonoma County to the south. I don't personally own a horse anymore, but when I did, I loved to go on trail rides.

I would take one of the girls with me; we would saddle up, and off we would go. We would start our ride on the service roads of our ranch that are nice and wide. They are great for riding side by side, so we could chat going along at a leisurely pace. If we wanted to veer off the dirt road, we could choose from many different trails. These trails are much more narrow than the road and would require us to travel along in single file, one horse following the other. We would start out on a cattle trail that is a wider and gentle path to follow. The cattle are looking for good grazing and like to stay out in the open in groups for security. As you ride up into the hills, the paths start to decrease in size. Some of them can get rather precarious due to the fact that they are paths made from either deer or wild pigs. The legs of these

animals are shorter and closer together, so the trail becomes
a tiny footpath. The deer and pig also travel over some rather
intense terrain, which can be a challenge to ride at times.

It often occurs to me that our walk as Christians is a lot like
these trail rides. Sometimes we have the pleasure of riding side by
side, where we can converse with our Lord. Other times one will
lead, and the other follow; conversation at this point is difficult;
I may have to speak with more intention being sure to keep my
eyes on the trail. At times, the trail is even and uneventful, and
other times, it is full of challenging terrain. My job is to keep on
the path and not stray from following my Lord; He knows the
way and is more than willing to show me. I mentioned yesterday
that hope and faith walk hand in hand. Well, here is another one
for you in the path of a Christian. Love and forgiveness must ride
the challenging trail of life together. Sometimes, they ride side by
side, and other times, the only way is to have one of them take
the lead.

Love and forgiveness. I sure enjoy this tandem experience
when I am on the receiving end. God's love and forgiveness
offered to me by the cross are easy to behold. The path of my love
for those who have trespassed or sinned against me is much more
difficult. I need to follow Jesus on my life's path, just like I will
follow a sure-footed horse on a trail of tough terrain. Do I shove
my way to the front, or do I allow Jesus to take that lead until I
learn the landscape of life?

> If we say we have fellowship with him while we walk
> in darkness, we lie and do not practice the truth. But
> if we walk in the light, as he is in the light, we have
> fellowship with one another, and the blood of Jesus his
> Son cleanses us from all sin. If we say we have no sin,
> we deceive ourselves, and the truth is not in us. If we

confess our sins, he is faithful and just to forgive us our sins and to cleanse us from all unrighteousness. If we say we have not sinned, we make him a liar, and his word is not in us.

First John 1:6-12 (ESV)

If you need to read this in your own Bible, do so before answering the following questions.

1. Who should we fellowship with as we walk this trail of life?

2. What is it that we should be careful not to lie to ourselves about?

3. If we confess our sins, what happens?

So as we can see from the verses above, we need to be honest about where we are in association to our relationship with God and other believers. In Luke 11:4 (AMP):

> "And forgive us our sins, for we ourselves also forgive everyone who is indebted to us [who has offended us or done us wrong]. And bring us not into temptation but rescue us from evil."

Do you know what the temptation is that Luke is referring to? Describe the temptation that he is speaking about:

Now, I want you to verify or prove your answer by looking up four cross-references. A cross-reference helps to explain by giving you other examples in the Bible of the same concept or incidence.

Matthew 26:45-46,

Matthew 18:35.

You should back up a little to the earlier verses to get the context of this one.

Mark 11:25.

James 1:13-15.

How did your first answer compare to the meaning of the cross-references? There are several good points; write those points here:

You just studied the Word of God! For some of you, this may have been the first time. Others of you may be accustomed to studying the Bible. Don't forget that Jesus challenged the woman at the well in John 4:21-25 to be confident in her knowledge of who it was that she worshiped. It is fulfilling to understand the meaning of the Bible; peace wraps itself around the knowledge and application of the Word of God.

Forgiveness is huge in God's balance of right and wrong. So we need to allow ourselves to fully wrap around our hearts its meaning and application. We seek God's love when we ask Jesus into our hearts. That love comes because of the humility and brokenness of asking forgiveness for our trespasses against God and His character. God is love and is willing to give the ultimate gift of love, His Son Jesus. Love and forgiveness side by side!

God has a path marked out for us to travel; our job is to follow. Are you allowing the Lord through His Holy Spirit to lead you on this trail? I am going to use the Amplified Bible again in this next verse because we live in a culture that has redefined right from wrong. Let me put it this way; there is great peril for anyone who alters the Word of God to fit their personal needs or agenda. Remember we talked about knowing God. If we redefine right from wrong, we are trying to fit God into something that He is not, and thus we will not really know God. So we need to look deeply into the Word and what it means.

> Confess to one another therefore your faults (your slips, your false steps, your offenses, your sins) and pray [also] for one another, that you may be healed and restored [to a spiritual tone of mind and heart]. The earnest (heartfelt, continued) prayer of a righteous man makes tremendous power available [dynamic in its working].
>
> James 5:16 (AMP)

I want that to settle into your heart. Let the "peace of God" wash over you. There is satisfaction when we love others by forgiving them like Jesus forgave you. It is huge to love others so profoundly. I want you to listen to the following carefully; if what you are forgiving is an abusive behavior of someone towards you, just because you forgive them does not mean that you should subject yourself to their abusive behavior. They are the unhealthy ones, and you need to separate yourself from them. If you are not sure of what to do in this situation, ask your pastor or a counselor for help. You may even need to seek legal assistance.

I want to give you a couple more scriptures to meditate on. Please look up Luke 6:35-37.

List three points that you learned from this part of God's Word.
Points:

1.

2.

3.

So what were the sins that were carried to and placed on the
cross for you? I know that mine were a full and heavy load! When
we fully comprehend this concept of forgiveness, we become
truly satisfied. Yet, the love that I received in return was beyond
measure. No scale could calculate its weight of influence on my
heart. If we are so graciously forgiven, how could we not pardon
others by taking our water jars and pouring out grace and mercy?

We need to take a bath in the living water of forgiveness;
living because Jesus did not stay on the cross or in the tomb
of death but rose to the heights of heaven in love for us. The
amazing aspect of this is that He has prepared an eternal home
for us to live in a side-by-side relationship with Him. This makes
my heart smile!

> Jesus said, "The first in importance is, 'Listen, Israel:
> The Lord your God is one; so love the Lord God with
> all your passion and prayer and intelligence and energy.'
> And here is the second: 'Love others as well as you love
> yourself.' There is no other commandment that ranks
> with these."
>
> Mark 12:30-31 (MSG)

Prayer

Bathe me, Lord, in Your living water of forgiveness so that I can love others according to the path that You have blazed for those who follow You. I want to fill my jar so full of love that forgiveness for others is just who I am in You! Thank You, Jesus, for going to the cross and bearing my sins. Amen.

WEEK SIX

Riding the Trail with Wisdom and Insight
Day Four

My brother and I were raised as children in the city, and neither of us expressed a love of horses that I could describe as a passion. But as we grew up, married, and settled our families, a parallel line developed in the love of equestrian pursuits. I lived in Northern California with a ranch influence, and he lived in Southern California with an English flare. My brother Kyle, his wife, Cora, and their girls took hours of lessons and perfected their knowledge of riding and the understanding of the horse. Kyle had an older mare that he just loved; she was sweet, but she was getting on in years. He and his wife went on a trail ride in the hills, and this was when their knowledge and training paid off big time! He was riding behind Cora when his mare lost her footing on some loose gravel, and Kyle and his mare went tumbling down a ravine. When Cora looked back, all she could see, as the cloud of dust settled, was his mare lying on her back, and Kyle was nowhere to be found. For my brother, an equally frightening experience was about to unfold. Kyle says that as he was taking in everything that happened in those few moments, he was looking around him, but it was dark and still.

Trying to figure out where he was, he began to process the events that had just happened. And then it registered in his mind where he was. Dust and dirt were everywhere, except right above his face, where there was brown hair that was moving in and out with each breath that his mare was taking. He was wedged in

239

a crevice of the ravine with his mare lying on her back, lodged on top of him. Then in the muffled distance, he heard his wife calling his name with definite stress in her voice. From her view, she neither saw nor heard my brother. As this dangerous situation came into focus, the skills and knowledge that they both had accumulated over the years developed into action.

His wife was able to successfully pull up and off the mare from my brother without crushing or stepping on him. Cora knew to pull the horse off of him at an angle so that the mare's feet could land at a downhill location. Unfortunately, here the footing was also loose gravel, and now she and the mare went tumbling further down the ravine, and Cora was the one who came out of this incidence with a fractured rib. But all in all, lessons were learned, skills were used, and all lived to ride again!

When things get difficult, it is our experience through knowledge that yields the confidence needed to continue with success. We could safely say there is satisfaction in knowing. Wisdom and insight did what was necessary; they, too, are riding this trail together.

Have you ever had to encounter a difficult choice or situation? When contemplating its solution, how did you come to your conclusion on how to go about its answer?

Cora did not have the luxury of time to decide what to do, but she had something else; she had Kyle's encouragement. Yes, my brother was actually under that horse, talking her through what needed to be done. Here was a huge problem. How do you get a 1,100-pound horse up and off of a person when it is lying on its back in a ravine on a hillside without crushing the man underneath? What was going on in this short period of time was that each of them was looking at this situation from a different angle. Each saw a task of equal magnitude that needed to be accomplished and in a timely fashion.

Paul, too, when in Ephesus, was looking at a situation from a different perspective for an answer. He also sought wisdom from someone with experience and knowledge, his Lord.

Let's read together and talk about how to seek understanding, the kind that gives strength and power. Please read Ephesians chapter 3. Paul had a desire to understand the mysteries of God concerning the new Gentile believers. He wanted to wrap his mind around a new concept for him. God's embracing other people into the kingdom was new and "not politically correct" in 60 AD. As we explore chapter three, I want to bring to your attention a few points on the following pages.

Point 1

God will reveal what He wants you to know.

> That is, the mystery made known to me by revelation, as I have already written briefly. In reading this, then, you will be able to understand my insight into the mystery of Christ.
>
> Ephesians 3:3-4 (NIV)

What are the mysteries about God and His creation that you are struggling to understand in your life?

I often pray for wisdom and understanding about my walk as a believer, but I have since added insight to that list. Insight is what we are straining to see clearly, to solve the unknown with understanding. We have talked about looking up into the heavens to see the magnificence of God. And now we take in His words in order to reveal His truths in our hearts. There are mysteries of God, those concepts about His nature, that we sometimes do not fully comprehend because God is God. We refer to this as His omniscience. He is all-knowing! So once again, don't forget to tap into the all-knowing source for the answers to the questions you ask.

Point 2

God has a plan, which includes a sequence of events. He reveals His mysteries and truths to us according to His timing. Look at Paul, for example. Paul was Judean by residence and a Pharisee by denomination. Hebrew by race, he came from the tribe of Benjamin. He is a citizen of Rome who, at God's exact timing, converted to being a follower of Jesus. Paul had all of the needed ingredients to be the one that God used to reveal His mystery, God's plan to incorporate the Jews and Gentiles into one body of believers.

People who lived in other times were not told that
secret. But now, through the Spirit, God has shown that
secret to his holy apostles and prophets. This is that
secret: that through the Good News those who are not
Jews will share with the Jews in God's blessing. They
belong to the same body, and they share together in the
promise that God made in Christ Jesus.

Ephesians 3:5-6 (NLT)

Did you catch that? It may help you to underline some
keywords. Please write out the secret.

Why was this such a mystery?

Point 3

God gives insight so we can help others to understand.

By God's special gift of grace given to me through his
power, I became a servant to tell that Good News. I am
the least important of all God's people, but God gave
me this gift—to tell those who are not Jews the Good
News about the riches of Christ, which are too great to
understand fully. And God gave me the work of telling
all people about the plan for his secret, which has been
hidden in him since the beginning of time. He is the
One who created everything.

Ephesians 3:7-9 (NCV)

Paul, well qualified to teach, recognizes with humility that "I am the least important" and considers himself the "worst of sinners." Because of Paul's persecution of the Christians before his miraculous conversion, he felt unworthy of the task before him. Paul knew that his ability to uncover the mysteries was a gift from God. The Lord was the One that empowered him with passion to tell others the "good news" about Jesus. You can read in more detail the 9th chapter of Acts.

Can you share a time when you experienced the empowering of the Holy Spirit in you or someone else for the edifying of others?

Have you ever had the thrill of sharing the plan of salvation with anyone?

Point 4

God's wisdom is multifaceted.

> His intent was that now, through the church, the
> manifold wisdom of God should be made known to the
> rulers and authorities in the heavenly realms, according
> to his eternal purpose that he accomplished in Christ
> Jesus our Lord. In him and through faith in him we
> may approach God with freedom and confidence. I ask
> you, therefore, not to be discouraged because of my
> sufferings for you, which are your glory.
>
> Ephesians 3:10-13 (NIV)

I am going to try to describe to you manifold wisdom. But I
also want to encourage you to truly think, pray, and meditate on
this concept for your own insight. Manifold wisdom is a way to
describe the multifaceted aspects of God's nature. Did you know
that God has many names that describe who He is? You, too, may
have many names; for example, I am Caprice, believer, customer,
friend, employee, mom, sister, wife, teacher, RN, or student. All
of these names define who I am from a different perspective.
Each of these roles requires wisdom and knowledge to get the
job done.

God's wisdom also has many perspectives. I want you to
envision a very large and dazzling diamond sitting in front of
you. So immense that you could walk up to it and peer into its
magnificence through one of its many facets. As you approach
this diamond, you realize that you can actually look into the
crystal clarity of this precious jewel from different angles. God is
like this diamond; we can peer into His splendor from different
directions, never ceasing to be amazed at His stunning deity. He
is so holy and pure that He reflects such radiance from the variety

of His nature that the word that comes to my mind is "glorious"! Yet Paul tells us, "We may approach God with freedom and confidence." Why?

Why would God, who is so stunning and spectacular, allow us to approach Him with questioning mysteries on our lips? Why would God, the essence of all knowledge, be so approachable? Why? Because God is love! A very simple answer. He loves you and created you to have a relationship with Him. Just like the woman at the well, who in her time and culture had no right to even be near a Jew, let alone conversing and asking questions. Yet, we see at that intimate moment with the Master a love that says to each of us, "I love you, and no question or history of who you are matters." Only the answered mystery that Jesus is God and went to the cross for you and me so we could share in His plan of unconditional love for us!

Prayer

Our prayer today is from me to you, from Paul's prayer in Ephesians 3:14-16 (NLT), "When I think of all this, I fall to my knees and pray to the Father, the Creator of everything in heaven and on earth. I pray that from his glorious, unlimited resources he will empower you with inner strength through his Spirit." Amen!

Now go and give insight to others about the good news!

Joy at the End of the Trail

Day Five

Trail rides are a blast! It seems a common longing in our hearts to be able to saddle up and ride into the sunset. There was a legendary cowboy team, Roy Rogers and Dale Evans-Rogers, that captured the hearts of many. As a couple, Roy and Dale had made many movies and even had a TV show. They loved Jesus and were always careful to teach right from wrong with a solid moral message in every production.

Dale wrote the following song:

"Happy Trails to You
Some trails are happy ones,
Others are blue.
It's the way you ride the trail that counts,
Here's a happy one for you.
Happy trails to you until we meet again.

Happy trails to you
 keep smilin' until then.
Who cares about the clouds when we're together?
Just sing a song and bring the sunny weather.
Happy trails to you 'till we meet again."
(music and lyrics by Dale Evans-Rogers)

This song became our ranch theme song. Corny as it sounds, when our children were young, if you came for a visit, you had an unusual treat in store when you departed from our home. We would all stand on the front porch to sing this song and wave goodbye to our dear friends. It was a grand time of life, full of joy and happy memories. Now, hold on here a second...didn't we ever have any heartaches? Yes, we did, but as I learned years ago, 2 Corinthians 10:5 (KJV):

> Casting down imaginations, and every high thing that exalteth itself against the knowledge of God, and bringing into captivity every thought to the obedience of Christ.

My pastor taught us years ago that happiness is based upon our circumstances, and joy comes from the Lord. It is an active choice that I make each day to have the joy of the Lord in my heart. I do this by lassoing every thought and wrapping what I know about God around it until I have the joy of the Lord evident in all that I do.

Read it here in 2 Corinthians 10:3-6 (MSG):

> The world is unprincipled. It's dog-eat-dog out there! The world doesn't fight fair. But we don't live or fight our battles that way—never have and never will. The tools of our trade aren't for marketing or manipulation, but they are for demolishing that entire massively corrupt culture. We use our powerful God-tools for smashing warped philosophies, tearing down barriers erected against the truth of God, fitting every loose thought and emotion and impulse into the structure of life shaped by Christ. Our tools are ready at hand for clearing the ground of every obstruction and building lives of obedience into maturity.

What will the tools of God help you to do? Make a list of the results of taking every thought captive from the translation of the Message.

We are going to take a look into Philippians, written by Paul while he was in prison. The prison term that he was serving at the time of this writing was not the Mamertine Prison. Instead, he was in what was known as house arrest. For many of you who are reading this, you may feel like you are under "house arrest"; life is not what you thought it would be. Are you a shut-in due to age or illness? Do you consider the marriage you are in as an imprisonment to someone who is not the one you thought they were? How about your source of employment? Is your employer demanding and unkind? Or more heartbreaking, were you the victim of abuse that haunts you to this day?

So many awful things happen in this world in our short time on this earth. But once again, God's love has a way to get through. Maybe another time, I can share my struggle to learn with confidence that God does care no matter what you did or what has happened to you. I have been the victim and the victimizer. I have learned and received God's love, grace, and mercy on both sides of the equation. This has allowed me to know true peace of mind and the joy of the Lord. I want to encourage you to take your thoughts and give them to the Lord to be washed by the living water. Read Philippians 4:4-15 in your Bible, and then we will review it together in different versions.

> Always be full of joy in the Lord. I say it again—rejoice! Let everyone see that you are considerate in all you do. Remember, the Lord is coming soon. Don't worry about anything; instead, pray about everything. Tell God what you need, and thank him for all he has done. Then you will experience God's peace, which exceeds anything we can understand. His peace will guard your hearts and minds as you live in Christ Jesus.
>
> Philippians 4:4-7 (NLT)

When I rejoice, the peace of the Lord washes over me and soothes my soul. And when I am at peace, a peace that comes from the source of God's love, I can do the above.

Reread the verse above, then draw a line from the left column to match the right. These are nine great applications to live by:

Fill up on the joy	be considerate
Remember	surpasses all understanding
Don't be distressed	about anything
Pray	from the Lord
Let God know	guards our hearts and minds
God's Peace	the Lord is coming soon
His peace	for all he has done
Whatever you do	about everything
Be thankful	your needs

If you are struggling with having a mind that has no joyful thoughts, there is always the course of seeking help from your pastor or a professional counselor. Don't let life continue on the negative any longer. Seek help for what is troubling you. Or, if you think it is just a bit of "mind over matter," you could take the above sentences, write them down on strips of paper, and put them places where you could read them as daily reminders. If you bind them to your memory and tether them to your heart, you will be amazed at the joy from the Lord that will capture you!

> Finally, my friends, keep your minds on whatever is true, pure, right, holy, friendly, and proper. Don't ever stop thinking about what is truly worthwhile and worthy of praise. You know the teachings I gave you, and you know what you heard me say and saw me do. So follow my example. And God, who gives peace, will be with you.
>
> Philippians 4:8-9 (CEV)

Paul tells us to follow his example; remember his example is being lived while he is under house arrest. I don't know about you, but I sometimes struggle to do these things. So what is pure, true, holy, and right? I know that if I sit down to a breakfast of pancakes, I much prefer to put pure maple syrup on them rather than something that is made to taste like maple syrup. Take a look sometime at the list of ingredients on a bottle of the fake stuff. I do enjoy the authentic.

Pure, holy, true, friendly, and proper; what do these words mean
to you?

Pure

Holy

True

Friendly

Proper

Paul tells us not to ever stop thinking about "what is truly
worthwhile and worthy of praise." Not to stop because if we
do, we will become distracted in our thinking. This is not
brainwashing in the negative sense, but a washing and satisfying
of our hearts and minds through the "peace of God." How
can I have peace if I pollute my heart and soul with violence,
pornography, bitterness, or hate? Actually, the list of what can
pollute a person's heart is back to "sIn." Our God is holy and
pure. If we are to be His children, we need to take out our lassoes
and rope our thoughts so they are like our Father's. We discover
these truths in His Word, the Bible.

> I rejoiced greatly in the Lord that at last you renewed
> your concern for me. Indeed, you were concerned, but
> you had no opportunity to show it. I am not saying this
> because I am in need, for I have learned to be content

whatever the circumstances. I know what it is to be in need, and I know what it is to have plenty. I have learned the secret of being content in any and every situation, whether well fed or hungry, whether living in plenty or in want. I can do all this through him who gives me strength. Yet it was good of you to share in my troubles.

Philippians 4:10-14 (NIV)

Sharing together through good and bad times is how a family, whether biological or as a church fellowship, should function. It is a process to fully understand the meaning of contentment, leaning into the Word, trusting others to help you on your path, and immersing yourself in the living water of God.

I think that the woman at the well experienced this washing and felt a true peace of heart and mind. This led to a hope that she was loved, forgiven, and then, an incredible joy followed! Such a joy that she is ready to leave behind the things of her world that had chipped away at her well-being. She was no longer in need of the "acorns of life" that had filled her empty world and jar. She now knows and is eager to share the good news.

Then, leaving her water jar, the woman went back to the town and said to the people, 'Come, see a man who told me everything I ever did. Could this be the Messiah?' They came out of the town and made their way toward him.

John 4:28-30 (NIV)

The woman at the well left her "water jar of the world" behind. Will you leave yours?

Prayer

Dear Lord,

Thank You, Lord, for loving me unconditionally!

Thank You for Your...

Word,

truth,

mercy,

grace,

peace,

hope,

encouragement,

and wisdom.

My list could, and should, go on and on!

But for today, I rest in You, knowing that Your love for me is eternal, and my job to love others is made easier knowing that You walk before me! Thank You for this time together with others in You; bless them, Father, and keep them tucked close to Your heart! Amen.

I WANT JESUS IN MY HEART

So Now What?

Look...Search...Seek

> Seek the Lord while He may be found (for salvation) while He is near.
>
> Isaiah 55:6 (AMP)

Admit...understand the trespasses against God, the emptiness, and the consequences of a life without Jesus.

> Repent, then, and turn to God, so that your sins may be wiped out, that times of refreshing may come from the Lord.
>
> Acts 3:19 (NIV)

> But if we confess our sins to God, he can always be trusted to forgive us and take our sins away.
>
> First John 1:9 (CEV)

> For everyone has sinned; we all fall short of God's glorious standard.
>
> Romans 3:23 (NLT)

> For the wages of sin is death, but the free gift of God (that is, His remarkable, overwhelming gift of grace to believers) is eternal life in Christ Jesus our Lord.
>
> Romans 6:23 (AMP)

Believe God...Believe in His Son Jesus and what He has done for us!

> For God so loved the world that he gave his one and
> only Son, that whoever believes in him shall not perish
> but have eternal life.
>
> John 3:16 (NIV)

> God loved the people of this world so much that he
> gave his only Son, so that everyone who has faith in him
> will have eternal life and never really die, God did not
> send his Son into the world to condemn its people. He
> sent him to save them!
>
> John 3:16-17 (CEV)

Tell someone...confess that you now walk in the truth of God's love for you!

> So you will be saved, if you honestly say, 'Jesus is Lord,'
> and if you believe with all your heart that God raised
> him from death. God will accept you and save you, if
> you truly believe this and tell it to others.
>
> Romans 10:9-10 (CEV)

Won't you pray to ask Jesus into your life? Take a hold of the Lord's hand and pray this prayer...

Dear Lord,

I admit that I have trespassed against You by all the actions and thoughts of my life that are not right. Those things that have in the past put me first and not You. I now want to change, to walk the rest of my life eternally with You! To turn away from the things that are wrong and not of You and Your holiness.

I believe, Father God, that Jesus is Your Son, sent to this earth to pay the price for me and my sins. Because of this, I would be forgiven, *and I am forgiven!* So, Lord, I am today asking You into my life to be my Lord. I am going to trust You from here on out In the precious and powerful name of Jesus, Amen!

What should I do next?

If you do not yet have your own personal Bible, now is the time to get one! Take your time and make sure that it is a version that is recognized as accurate and that you can read and understand.

Seek other Christians and a church.

Pray for God's guidance, and He will give it to you!

And don't forget to help others to find their way to the Lord.

Then, leaving her water jar, the woman went back to the town and said to the people, 'Come, see a man who told me everything I ever did. Could this be the Messiah?' They came out of the town and made their way toward him.

John 4:28-30 (NIV)

ABOUT THE AUTHOR

Caprice Candace first came to know that Lord when she was ten years old; then, at the age of twenty-three, she rededicated her life to the Lord. She describes those thirteen years as very similar to the woman at the well, "At the tender age of ten, I desperately wanted to know Jesus as my Savior. But I was not willing, due to lack of full understanding, to make a complete commitment of unadulterated loyalty. The years that followed were miserable and empty as I tried to fill my water jar with anything I could cram in there. At the age of twenty-three, I finally got the full image of who God was and who He wanted me to be. I then knew that I not only needed a savior, but I needed to recognize who was the Lord of my life and live according to His plan, not mine." Shortly after her commitment to follow with all of her heart, the Lord led her and her husband on an amazing adventure in ministry.

Caprice has had the opportunity to serve the Lord in many different ways. She has taught Sunday school, served as youth director in Student Ministries for thirteen years with her husband, was the priority team leader for missions and women at the church that she and her family helped plant, Crossroads Christian Church in Ukiah, CA. Having been a member of CSBC for twenty-five years, she states that one of her greatest joys is having had the privilege to serve on medical teams during times of disaster. She served in Indonesia post the 2004 tsunami, Haiti, New Orleans, and Guatemala with IMB and NAMB. She has also served in public arenas in disaster relief as a chaplain with NAMB.

As a registered nurse, she received training in limited obstetrical ultrasound and the opportunity of sharing with women some of the first glimpses of their unborn children, aiding their decision for choosing life at a local PRC.

She and her husband raised their five children in Northern California on a ranch in a rural coastal valley. All five were homeschooled until they entered into four-year Christian universities and have married wonderful Christian spouses. She says one of her greatest joys is the title of "grandma" to twelve grandchildren!

She states that her prayer for the last several years has been to have "epic impact" for the Lord, "I want to be like the woman at the well, leaving my water jar behind and sharing with those willing to listen. I want to help others on this road of discovery to open their eyes that they might see, their ears that they might hear, their minds to understand, and hearts to receive the living water of eternal life for themselves. So they will begin to understand and thirst no more."

Happy Trails

CPSIA information can be obtained
at www.ICGtesting.com
Printed in the USA
JSHW041111210222
23137JS00001B/5